KENNETH SAWYER GOODMAN

A Chronology
&
Annotated Bibliography

KENNETH SAWYER GOODMAN

A Chronology
&
Annotated Bibliography

Compiled and Edited by
DENNIS BATORY KITSZ

THE NEWBERRY LIBRARY
Chicago, Illinois

First edition

Copyright © 1983 by
The Newberry Library
All rights reserved
Printed in the United States of America

Library of Congress Cataloging in Publication Data

Kitsz, Dennis Batory, 1949–
Kenneth Sawyer Goodman, a chronology & annotated bibliography.

1. Goodman, Kenneth Sawyer, 1883-1918–Bibliography.
2. Goodman, Kenneth Sawyer, 1883-1918–Chronology.
I. Title.
Z8355.43.K57   1983   [PS3513.525]   016.812'52   83-4054
ISBN 0-911028-25-0

LOGOTYPE OF THE STAGE GUILD, PUBLISHER OF
KENNETH SAWYER GOODMAN'S PLAYS
(Printed with permission of The Stage Guild, Inc.)

In memory of

Kenneth Sawyer Goodman Dewey

who followed in his
grandfather's footsteps
and for the other talented
grandchildren and
great-grandchildren of

Kenneth Sawyer Goodman

WILLIAM OWEN GOODMAN RESIDENCE AT 5026
GREENWOOD AVENUE, CHICAGO, ILLINOIS. (Right)
KENNETH SAWYER GOODMAN'S ROOM

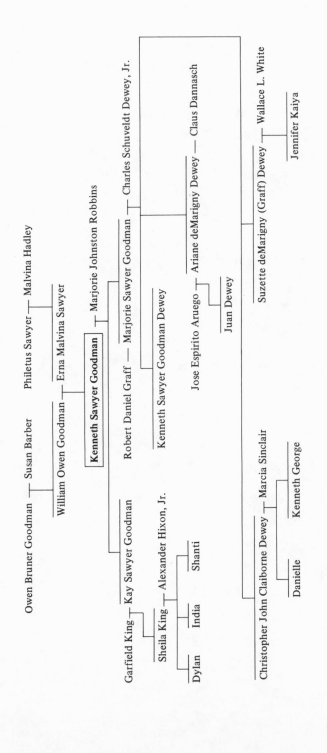

TABLE OF CONTENTS

THE PRINCETON TIGER

K·S·GOODMAN '06

Vol. 16, No. 8   Price 25 Cents   April, 1906

COVER FOR *THE PRINCETON TIGER*, APRIL 1906 (M375)

FOREWORD

Kenneth Sawyer Goodman was a leading figure in the cultural life of Chicago, particularly the "little theater" movement, during the period immediately preceding America's entry into World War I. Goodman managed to work extensively in the theater despite the demands of a full-time business career. He wrote one-act plays which set standards then, and are still played today. *The Game of Chess* appears in anthologies, including Bennett Cerf's *Thirty Famous One Act Plays* and *Reading and Staging the Play*, by John Gassner. Other plays, including *Dust of the Road*, continue to be performed, acted, and used in teaching as classic examples of the one-act genre.

Goodman's bibliography appears at this time of renewed interest in the early decades of the twentieth century. This was a time of creative excitement in Chicago. Harriet Monroe's magazine, *Poetry*, was bringing European and avant-garde poets, including Ezra Pound and T.S. Eliot, to Chicago readers. The Trustees of the Art Institute had the courage to open the door of their museum to the Armory Show. Charles MacArthur and Ben Hecht were working on *The Daily News*, which led them to collaborate on the play, *The Front Page*. Collaborating with Hecht also was Kenneth Sawyer Goodman. The Arts Club, which opened in shared office space in the Fine Arts Building, organized a series of avant-garde exhibitions, bringing many European artists who were unknown in the United States to the attention of Chicago for the first time. It was in this effervescent atmosphere that Kenneth Sawyer Goodman wrote and produced his one-act plays.

❡

Kenneth Sawyer Goodman was born in Chicago on September 19, 1883, the only child of William Owen Goodman and the former Erna Malvina Sawyer. He descended from pioneer stock through both parents.

His grandfather, Philetus Sawyer, went from Crown Point, N.Y., where he was born, to Wisconsin to make his fortune. He succeeded. There is a family story that, at seventeen, he borrowed $100 from his brother to "buy his time," in other

xi

ENTRANCE TO THE KENNETH SAWYER GOODMAN MEMORIAL THEATRE
(FROM *BULLETIN OF THE ART INSTITUTE OF CHICAGO*, OCTOBER 1925)

words, to be released from working for his father. By the age of thirty, he had saved $2,000 which he used to move to Wisconsin in 1847 and to buy his first piece of land from the Government at $1.25 an acre. He was elected to the House of Representatives in 1861 and, at the time of young Kenneth's birth, had been U.S. Senator from Wisconsin for two years.

Owen Bruner Goodman, Kenneth's other grandfather, was a descendant of French Huegenots who had fled France in the sixteenth century at the time of the Massacre of St. Bartholomew. Born in 1812, this native of Lancaster, Pennsylvania, worked for a Columbia lumber mill nearby. He and his wife braved the rigors of sailing up the Susquehanna River to Williamsport, as far as navigation went. They then went on by ox cart to a wilderness log house in Pike Mills. From the logging operations there, Goodman followed the rafts floating back down the Susquehanna to the Columbia sawmill. His wife returned to Columbia periodically to bear their children. It was here that William Owen Goodman was born. From Pennsylvania, Owen went to Wisconsin, where he continued to pursue his career as a lumberman. Much later, in 1908, the town of Goodman, Wisconsin, was named after him.

Owen's son, Will, followed him in the lumber business, eventually becoming the partner of Philetus Sawyer. The firm of Sawyer, Goodman & Co. was thus formed. In 1878, Will Goodman married his partner's daughter, Erna, who was twelve years his junior. To open an office for the family lumber business, Will and his wife moved to Chicago, where they lived in a house on South Michigan Avenue. It was in this house, a present from the bride's parents, that Kenneth was born.

Kenneth—or K, as he was known to family and friends for the rest of his life— grew up on Chicago's South Side in a spacious house on Greenwood Avenue where he and his young friends staged and acted in "plays." After attending school in Chicago, he went to the Hill School in Pottstown, Pennsylvania in 1898. There is evidence, in the Hill School newspaper, that K was already writing and drawing.

In 1902, he went on to Princeton and began writing seriously (and humorously) for *The Princeton Tiger*. He became its editor and continued to contribute drawings, poems, and stories. During this period, he came to admire greatly and seek advice from Christian Gauss, who eventually steered K away from poetry and into playwriting. It was probably Dean Gauss who suggested that K Goodman be asked to return after his graduation in 1906 to teach in the English Department at Princeton, a proposal K considered at the time.

Although K decided not to teach, soon after graduation he announced to his family that he wished to write plays for a career. Although his parents were already active collectors and patrons of the arts, there was concern that their son should wish to become a full-time playwright. It had always been assumed that he, an only son, would go into the family business.

Perhaps to give himself time to think over his choice of career, K accompanied his parents on a leisurely tour. Diaries written by K and by his father, and some amusing photographs, chronicle this 1907 odyssey to Europe and Egypt. On returning to the United States, K made the difficult decision to enter the family business; he was sent to Wisconsin for a year's training and experience. Although there was little doubt in K's mind about his desire to pursue a career in the theater, he took seriously his business responsibility.

While working for the lumber company in Chicago, K became deeply involved in the cultural life of the city. He was named Director of the Art Institute's Prints Department, and the Annual Report of 1910-11 states, "The Department of Prints, under the Directorship of Kenneth Sawyer Goodman, has been much more active than before."

During this period, K was also writing, directing, and sometimes acting in plays. A scrapbook kept between 1911 and 1917 (now at the Newberry Library) documents the theatrical activity—much of it quite experimental—in Chicago during these years. It was then that K Goodman began to dream and, in fact, to formulate plans for a theater which would combine a repertory company with a dramatic arts school taught by actors in the company. It was not until after his death in 1918, however, that K's dream was fulfilled by his parents. They gave the Kenneth Sawyer Goodman Theatre at the Chicago Art Institute in his memory. The theatre opened in 1925.

¶

This bibliography, I hope, will make it possible to understand the development of one creative artist who reflected both the temper of his times and his reactions to the fortunate circumstances of his life. The promise he showed as a playwright was never fulfilled; he died as a World War I naval officer in Chicago at age thirty-four, during the influenza epidemic of 1918.

Initially, it was my intention to provide a simple checklist and chronology of Kenneth Sawyer Goodman's published works. However, when James Wells of The Newberry Library expressed interest in having the literary and artistic works, published and unpublished, returned to Chicago, a search was begun to bring together all the extant work.

To this end, I asked a young artist, Dennis Kitsz, to help with this project. As work progressed, more and more original, unpublished writings and drawings came to light, some of them rescued from old bank files scheduled for destruction. Dennis Kitsz's patience, scholarship, and involvement in this project realized my personal desire to preserve a record of my father's achievements and to make the best of them better known and available.

Marjorie Sawyer Goodman Graff
Far Hills, New Jersey

To Harriet who has known all of us for a long time + who continues to be an inspiration. Much, much love Marjo

ACKNOWLEDGMENTS

The preparation of this bibliography of the works of Kenneth Sawyer Goodman has been a distinct privilege and great pleasure. Enthusiasm and cooperation were received from all sources, and the discovery of many of the lost Goodman works has been a rewarding experience.

I would like to thank Mr. James M. Wells, vice president of The Newberry Library in Chicago, for guidance and help in assessing the needs of future researchers; also, my thanks to his fine staff. Mr. David Dangler of the Northern Trust Company provided me a warm welcome in Chicago, and helped me locate many of the missing manuscripts; my thanks to him.

Also, my appreciation goes to the staff of *The Princeton Tiger* and the Firestone Library at Princeton University; to the staff of The New York Public Library Theatre Collection at Lincoln Center; to Mr. Harold Graves, for astute appraisal of the importance of the manuscripts; to Peggy Dee Horwitz, who turned mounds of cards into neatly typed sheets; to Leah Sloshberg and her staff at The New Jersey State Museum, for lending equipment and encouragement; to Barbara Palfy, for coordinating publication of the work; and to the family and friends of Kenneth Sawyer Goodman.

Finally, I thank Marjorie Goodman Graff, whose foresight and dedication will cause the outstanding works of her father to be read, viewed, and appreciated by a wider audience.

D.B.K.

Kenneth Sawyer Goodman with his Daughter,
Marjorie Sawyer Goodman, 1918

PART ONE
A
Selected
Chronology

DRAWING FOR *EPHRAIM AND THE WINGED BEAR* (M80)

CHRONOLOGY

1910   November 6-9: Working on *Goya*

November 21-December 1: Rehearsals for *Goya*

December 7: *Goya* produced

December 16-18: Work on *The Masque of Quetzal's Bowl*

1911   January 6: *The Masque of Quetzal's Bowl* produced

January 28: Decision to write *The Daimio's Head*

February 28: *The Daimio's Head* produced

April 1: *A Revision of Salome* produced

April 16: First mention of *Immigrant League*

April 23: Work begins on *A Pageant for Independence Day*

July 4: *A Pageant for Independence Day* produced

August 31: First mention of *Wine of Luck*

November 3: First mention of manuscript for "a French play"
   (*Le Course du Flambeau*)

November 11: Elected Director of the Art Students League

November 23: Work on *Ryland*

1912   January 10: *Ryland* is completed

February 29-March 1: Rehearsals for *Ryland*

March 7: *Ryland* produced

March 11: *Passing of the Torch* (*Le Course du Flambeau*) produced

March 14: *The Masque of Montezuma* in rehearsal

KENNETH SAWYER GOODMAN, MARCH 15, 1885

March 19-20: Work on "Helen of Troy" play

April 23-29: "Judas Play" (*Dust of the Road*) in progress

June 12: Kenneth Sawyer Goodman marries Marjorie Robbins

June 18-July 11: Work in progress on "new Pierrot play"
(*The Wonder Hat*)

July 4: The Goodmans attend "a baseball game and suffragette parade"

September 2: Finishes a Pierrot play (second?)

October 4: Begins a "third Pierrot play"

October 15: Attempted assassination of Theodore Roosevelt takes place

November 12: Looking for material for a "Byzantine Masque"
(*Caesar's Gods*)

November 24: Finishes *A Game of Chess*

December 16: Cast discussion for *Dancing Dolls*

December 18-19: Rehearsals of *Dancing Dolls*

December 19: The Goodmans hear Schumann-Heinck in
Tristan und Isolde

December 22: Finishes scenario of "Mardi Gras Masque"

1913   January [?] : *Dust of the Road* first produced

January 6-14: Plans for Byzantine Masque

January 30-31: Byzantine Masque (*Caesar's Gods*) in rehearsal

February 4: *Caesar's Gods* produced

February 9: The Goodmans leave on a trip to California and Hawaii

February 11: Work on *Holbein in Blackfriars* (*Holbein in Cheapside*)

March 8: *Holbein in Blackfriars* produced

March 15: *Dust of the Road* first officially produced

April 26: The Goodmans return from their trip

April 27: First mention of *Back of the Yards*

May 5: New draft of *Holbein in Blackfriars* is finished

June 2: Work begins on *At the Edge of the Wood*

June 14: First version of *At the Edge of the Wood* is produced

June 29: Finishes *Back of the Yards*

July 16: Finishes "Tempest in the Teapot" (=*Red Flag* [?] cf. March 31, 1914)

July 25: Work on article on pageants for the Play Book

August 6–18: Writing *Queens Tragedy*

August 19: Begins *Behind the Black Cloth*

August 27: Writing new short play

September 4: At Duck Island, Trenton, N.J.

October 16: "[B. Iden] Payne is enthusiastic over *Ryland*"

November 11: *The Game of Chess* produced

November 13–19: Working on *The Wonder Hat*

November 17: Begins work on a new play, an "artificial comedy"

November 18: *The Game of Chess* "officially" produced

November 21: Finishes draft of *Barbara*

December 5: Rehearsal for *Barbara*

December 9: *Barbara* produced

December 15–17: Work on Christmas play (*Ephraim and the Winged Bear*)

December 20: Looking for material for a "Crusade masque"

December 22: Decides against producing *Ephraim and the Winged Bear*

December 23–26: Work on scenario of the Medieval Masque (*Rainald and the Red Wolf*)

1914　January 13: Proofs of *The Game of Chess*

February 3: Work on *Rainald and the Red Wolf*

February 9: Marjorie Sawyer Goodman born

February 20: Rehearsals for *Rainald and the Red Wolf*

February 24: *Rainald and the Red Wolf* produced

March 6–17: Work on *The Toy Maker*

March 9–11: Work begins on *A Man Can Only Do His Best*

March 19: Drama article appears in The Nation

March 23: Rights assigned to *The Game of Chess*

March 24: Marjorie Sawyer Goodman christened

Kenneth Sawyer Goodman as "Waldevic," 1891

March 29: Work begins on *Behind the Black Cloth*

March 31-April 1: Work on "Tempest in a Teapot" (*The Red Flag*)

April 2: *The Red Flag* is finished

May 16: Draft of *At the Edge of the Wood*

May 18: Finishes *At the Edge of the Wood*

May 29: St. Louis Masque by Thomas Wood Stevens is performed

June 13: *At the Edge of the Wood* produced

June 15: *Dancing Dolls* produced

June 24: Working on "a new play"

July 6: *A Man Can Only Do His Best* produced

July 29-August 4: Working on cover for *Ephraim and the Winged Bear*

August 1: "European war scare" noted

August 6: Finishes draft of "How Like a Man" (*The Green Scarf*)

August 30: Corrects proofs for *Back of the Yards* and
Ephraim and the Winged Bear

September 5: *The Educated Anteater* produced

September 26: Receives proofs for *Masques of East and West* and
declares them "in bad shape"

October 3: B. Iden Payne reads *The Home Coming* and
The Poem of David

October 4: New ending for *The Poem of David*

October 27: Finishes redraft of ending of *The Poem of David*

November 5: Begins redrafting *Death Watch* by Ben Hecht

November 17: Revises script of *The Wonder Hat;* finishes redraft of
Death Watch; writes rough draft of *The Egg and the Hen;* completes
outline and work on "Canadian Melodrama"

November 27: Finishes corrected draft of *A Man Can Only Do His Best*

1915   February 12: Finishes work on *The Two Lamps*

February 19-20: Work on *The Egg and the Hen*

February 24-26: *The Egg and the Hen* in revision

March 1: Finishes *The Egg and the Hen*

March 5: *Back of the Yards* produced

KENNETH SAWYER GOODMAN,
ca. 1895

March 31: Begins work on *The Hand of Siva*

May [?]: *The Wonder Hat* produced

June 16: *The Poem of David* produced

June 17-September 21: Goodman begins painting

July 19-24: Working with Ben Hecht on "For Old Glory"

July 23: Working on draft of "a new short play"

July 26: Planning prologue for Durot series

July 28-August 1: Working on prologue for Durot series

August 3: Finishes Durot prologue

August 4: Draft of Durot prologue corrected with B. Iden Payne

September 27-October 8: Working on "a marionette play"

November 30: Hecht and Marie Armstrong elope

December 9: Finishes draft of *An Idyll of the Shops*

December 23: Finishes draft of "How Like A Man" (*The Green Scarf*)

1916   February 20-22: "Fort Wayne Pageant" in the works (*The Glorious Gateway of the West*)

February 24: *Henri Durot, Master Spy* produced

March 27: Casino movie (*Cousin Jim*) first mentioned

April: Work on Fort Wayne Pageant

April 3-May 2: Casino movie in progress

June 2: Opening of *Cousin Jim;* Goodman does not attend

June 5: The Players Workshop produces *The Home Coming* and *The Wonder Hat*

June 7: Goodman attends a suffragette parade; also sees *Cousin Jim* and makes changes

June 12: *Cousin Jim* "officially" produced

June 14: Publication of *A Man Can Only Do His Best*

July 8-11: Working on model stage furniture

July 10: *The Red Flag* and *An Idyll of the Shops* produced

July 19: *The Red Flag* "officially" produced

November 21: The Goodmans hear Galli-Curci in *Lucia di Lammermoor*

KENNETH SAWYER GOODMAN, 1899

December 14: *An Idyll of the Shops* "officially" produced

December [?] : *Ephraim and the Winged Bear* produced

1917   January 3: *Ephraim and the Winged Bear* "officially" produced

May 26: Goodman enters the U.S. Naval Reserve

September 16: *The Egg and the Hen* produced

February 12: *The Hero of Santa Maria* produced

1918   April 5: Goodman appointed Lieutenant 4th Class

November 29: Kenneth Sawyer Goodman dies in Chicago at the home of his parents, 1355 Astor Street

December 11: Goodman's obituary appears in the *Princeton Alumni Weekly*, 19:11, p. 217

1920   February 21: *The Green Scarf* produced

1923   February [?] : *Behind the Black Cloth* produced

HEADPIECE FOR THE *PRINCETON BRIC-A-BRAC,*
1905 (M376b)

PART TWO
Annotated Bibliography

EARLY DRAWING, PRIOR TO 1902[X]

GUIDE

F or the purposes of this bibliography, the works of Kenneth Sawyer Goodman have been divided into sections by genre. Within each section, entries are alphabetically arranged, and each entry is assigned a code number (e.g., T10). The numbering, although consecutive, is spaced to allow for future inclusion of as yet undiscovered material. The coding is based on genre:

D	Diaries
M	Miscellany (letters, photographs, drawings, etc.)
P	Poetry
S	Short stories, articles, etc.
T	Theatrical works

	MEW	Masques of East and West
	MQC	More Quick Curtains
	QC	Quick Curtains
	WH	Wonder Hat

The collection of Kenneth Sawyer Goodman's works listed here is housed in The Newberry Library, 60 West Walton Street, Chicago, Illinois 60610, except where noted:

AZ	University of Arizona Library, Tucson, Arizona 85717
NYPL	Theatre Collection, The New York Public Library at Lincoln Center, 111 Amsterdam Avenue, New York, New York 10023
PUL	Firestone Library, Princeton University, Princeton, New Jersey 08540
X	Family collection of Marjorie Sawyer Goodman Graff, including ancillary matter in the form of photographs, photograph negatives, and personal memorabilia regarding Kenneth Sawyer Goodman, his forebears and progeny

Additional material may be found at The Goodman Theatre Center, 200 South Columbus Avenue, Chicago, Illinois; the Theatre Collection of the Chicago Public Library, 425 North Michigan Avenue, Chicago, Illinois 60611; and in the files of *The Princeton Tiger* at Princeton University, Princeton, New Jersey.

A REVISION OF SALOME!! OR, WHY YOUNG MEN LEAVE HOME. PRESENTED BY

THEATRICAL WORKS

SUMMARIES

At the Edge of the Wood

This masque was written specifically for the purpose of calling attention to the need to save natural areas from the ravages of progress, and involves a faun who pleads with an Indian, a pioneer and a builder, before coming across a friend willing to help preserve sections of natural wilderness.

Back of the Yards

A rough-hewn drama, in which a police sergeant and a priest meet following the shooting death of a neighborhood youth, and progressing through ever-deepening moral crises as the men find their favorite youngster involved.

Barbara

This light social comedy presents the cunning Barbara who, in attempting to steal a few personal trinkets from the home of the wealthy Archibald, bungles her way into a promise of marriage and high position.

Behind the Black Cloth

In this classic melodrama, Vera Pope, illegitimate daughter of a wealthy and now-deceased gentleman, makes unpleasant discoveries in the sanatorium in which her father died; through the perceptions of a newspaper reporter, she finds her claims to inheritance are unexpectedly and mysteriously difficult.

17

Caesar's Gods

Julian, Emperor of the East, is confronted by a choice between the old pagan gods of his ancestors, who give signs of great conquest, and Christianity, which gives virtually no signs or spells; the crux of his dilemma is presented in this masque.

The Daimio's Head

A masque in which O Toyo San sets out on a mission to avenge the demeaning death of her father, and, under the protection of a goblin and a samurai, successfully obtains the head of the Daimio to place on her father's grave.

Dancing Dolls

Four members of a comic theater company begin to express dissatisfaction with their lot in life, just as chance provides opportunity to a poultry farmer and his sister who have a desire to be entertainers and forsake their farm; a farce ensues when the transactions begin to take place.

Dust of the Road

Basically a morality play, this drama presents the ever-penitent Judas in the garb of a wandering old man, who happens upon the home of a middle-aged couple as they plan to cheat a trusting friend out of his inheritance.

The Educated Anteater

This is a fragment of light social comedy in which an anteater is trained by a rather difficult young child, and a master of ceremonies bemuses the audience with inept trickery.

The Egg and the Hen

This is a study of Jewish life in the ghetto in Chicago at the turn of the century, wherein the child, for the first time in school, causes pain and havoc within her family, a family that has sacrificed to send her there.

Ephraim and the Winged Bear

This play is a variant on the Dickens Christmas Story, as Ephraim Bumsteeple finds his dimly lit holiday home invaded by local low-life and a winged bear, all bent on making Ephraim have a good time in spite of himself.

The Game of Chess

A classic tale of a harried czarist Governor who believes his wits are leaving him, and a revolutionary peasant whose assassination attempt reassures the Governor that he is indeed in as fine a form as ever. This game is the height of contrived melodrama, and has been accepted as one of the prime examples of one-act play-writing.

The Green Scarf

A man and a woman meeting on a park bench in the early hours of the morning set the scene for an unsuccessful mutual suicide, replete with social commentary and sexual stereotypes.

The Hero of Santa Maria

The Spanish-American War is the time of this tragedy in which Nathan Fisher's son is killed, and is to receive a hero's honors; Nathan is put in an unfortunate position when his son turns up alive just before the ceremonies in which Nathan will have what is certain to be the only proud moment of his life.

Herring's Luck

From the playbill: "Mr. Wilson, having been Mayor of Chicago until 1915, is forced by ill health to take a vacation. His daughter, Irene, a militant suffragette, seizes control in his absence, becomes mayor, appoints her female friends to office, and disenfranchises all the men."

Holbein in Blackfriars

A farce in which Hans Holbein, imported from Germany to England to please the nobility, is commissioned to paint the portrait of Ann of Cleves, soon to marry Henry VIII; concealed identities and concealed paintings eventually lead to frustrations all around.

The Home Coming

Violinist Harold Silver, né Silverman, returns home to visit his parents after several years in Europe where he has established world fame; this character study reveals the self-interest of all the characters, and the tragedy inherent in their dreams and expectations.

19

An Idyll of the Shops

Set in a turn-of-the-century sweatshop, this tragedy presents a view of personal pride in a world where shop owner Max Bloom must struggle to survive on the shoulders of his workers; love, friendships and loyalties find they must wait.

A Man Can Only Do His Best

A quack doctor and his assistant are stuck without passports in a town under seige; a farce ensues as the assistant manages to get passports for three instead of two, and officialdom, scoundrels and lovers all try to claim a place out-of-town.

The Masque of Montezuma

Huitzil, the Aztec war god, has been long unsated by blood under the peaceful rule of Montezuma; however, the Spaniards under Cortez make their entrance into the sacred city, and Huitzil gets his revenge as once again there is the blood of war.

The Masque of Quetzal's Bowl

An old artificer is disturbed from his work fixing ancient museum pieces by a gentleman inquiring about cups, bowls or other drinking vessels and replete with stories of the power of such vessels to recall the past when filled with wine; the old man tests this thesis when the gentleman leaves, and a great Aztec ritual takes place.

The Parting

Spies and counterspies form the basis of this melodrama, in which an innocent lover is caught in a web of international loyalties and wartime cruelties when she finds herself used and cast aside by the man she believed loved her.

The Poem of David

An old man dreams of successful marionette plays, but these have been supplanted in popularity by moving pictures, and, unbeknownst to him in his blindness, his children have had to mortgage home and theater to continue his dream of a marionette play called the Poem of David.

Rainald and the Red Wolf

The medieval town of Lavayne has been invaded and taken over by Waldemar, who, with his Black Company, holds sway even over the Church; the Lord Rainald is pre-

20

sumed lost in the Crusades, but as his Lady is to be married to the evil Waldemar, he reappears in disguise in a miracle play.

The Red Flag

Colin Weyland finds himself breaking loose from the imperious Mrs. Swanbridge, his mother-in-law, and begins to advise his sister, the maid and all the others; unfortunately, destiny's comic hand makes Mrs. Swanbridge the victor *in absentia*.

A Revision of Salome

A burlesque in which audience, musicians, actors and stagehands participate, this Salome contains no plot, characterization or message; it is a pre-slapstick study on the order of a confused minstrel show.

Ryland

William Ryland is found on the day before he is to be hanged for forgery, and he uses every manner of deceit and trickery, including play on the sensitivities of his wife and an old lover, to gain his freedom.

The Wonder Hat

A harlequinade, in which the traditional magic slipper combines with a magic hat in a light spoof of spells, magic, love and invisibility; a classic Pierrot play.

SELECTED REVIEWS,
REFERENCES, AND COMMENTARY

Back of the Yards

Premiere: March 15, 1915; Lake Forest College, Garrick Club
No reviews available.

Barbara

Premiere: December 9, 1913; Fine Arts Theatre, Chicago
Reviews:
Chicago Daily News, December 10, 1913
Chicago Evening Post, December 10, 1913

CÆSAR'S GODS

GODS

A
BYZANTINE
MASQVE

BY·THOMAS·WOOD·STEVENS·AND·KENNETH·SAWY·
ER·GOODMAN·AND·GIVEN·BY·THE·ART·STVDEN
·TS·LEAGVE·OF·CHICAGO·FEBRVARY· FOVR·ONE·THOVSAND·NINE·
·HVNDRED·THIRTEEN

H·C·KIEFER

COVER OF THE PUBLISHED EDITION OF *CAESAR'S GODS*, 1913 (T50)

Chicago Tribune, December 17, 1913
Chicago Journal, December 17, 1913
Chicago Record-Herald, December 17, 1913
Boston Transcript, June 23, 1914

Cousin Jim

Scenario by C.W. Hitchcock, Kenneth S. Goodman and John T. McCutcheon.
No reviews available.

The Daimio's Head

Premiere: February 28, 1911; Art Student's League, Art Institute of Chicago
Musical setting by Harold E. Hammond
Advance notice:
Chicago Sunday Tribune, February 12, 1911
Review:
Chicago Evening Post, March 7, 1911
Other important performances:
Shrove Tuesday, 1915; Edgeworth Club, Sewickley, Pa.

Dancing Dolls

Premiere: August 15, 19[13?] ; Lakeside Players, Lakeside, Michigan
Reviews:
Pittsburgh Gazette Times, June 15, 1914
Pittsburgh Chronicle Telegraph, June 15, 1914; performance at the Carnegie In-
stitute of Technology, Department of Dramatic Arts, June 14, 1914

Dust of the Road

Premiere: March 15, 1913; Wisconsin Dramatic Society, Davidson Theatre,
Milwaukee, Wisconsin
Premiere also listed in another source as: February 28, 19[13?] ; Wisconsin
Dramatic Society, Fuller Opera House, Madison, Wisconsin
Reviews:
Milwaukee Sentinel, March 15, 1913
Milwaukee Free Press, March 15, 1913
Review of the publication:
The New York Times, August 3, 1913

Game of Chess

Premiere: November 18, 1913; Fine Arts Theatre, Chicago Theatre Society;
Directed by B. Iden Payne
Reviews:
Chicago Daily News, November 19, 1913
Chicago Examiner, November 19, 1913
Chicago Inter Ocean, November 19, 1913
Chicago Journal, November 19, 1913
Chicago Record-Herald, November 23, 1913
Chicago Tribune, November 19, 1913
Boston Transcript, December 4, 1913
Indianapolis News, February 24, 1914
Los Angeles Graphic, June 20, 1914
St. Paul Minnesota Pioneer, August 2, 1914

Goya

Premiere: December 7, 1910; Men's Life Class Association, Fullerton Hall, Art
Institute of Chicago
No reviews available.

Henri Durot Master Spy

combines a prologue (now lost) with *The Hand of Siva, The Two Lamps* and an
epilogue (also lost).
The prologue includes Henry Durrow, Florence, Jague, Reinhart, Wallpenny,
Wiley and others.
The epilogue includes Durrow, Florence and Wiley.
Premiere: February 24, 1916; Schenley Theatre, Pittsburgh, Pennsylvania, "un-
der the auspices of the War Relief Committee of the Carnegie Institute of
Technology"
No reviews available.

The Hero of Santa Maria

Premiere: February 12, 1917; Washington Square Players, New York City
No reviews available.

Herrings Luck

adapted by John B. Anderson and Kenneth Sawyer Goodman.
No reviews available.

Holbein in Blackfriars
Holbein in Cheapside

Premiere: March [May?] 8, 1913; Chicago Society of Etchers, Art Students'
League, Art Institute of Chicago
No reviews available.

The Home Coming

Premiere: June 5-10, 1916; Players Workshop, Hyde Park, Chicago
No reviews available.

An Idyll of the Shops

Documentation conflicts on premieres.
July 10-15, 1916; Players Workshop, Hyde Park, Chicago
December 11-16, 1916; Players Workshop
No reviews available.

Julian the Apostate
Caesar's Gods

Premiere: February 4, 1913; Art Students' League, Art Institute of Chicago
Musical setting by George A. Colburn.
No reviews available.

A Man Can Only Do His Best

Premiere: August 15, 19[?] ; Lakeside Players, Lakeside, Michigan
or: July 10-15, 1916; Players Workshop, Hyde Park, Chicago
Review:
New York Review, July 25, 1914

Masque
At the Edge of the Wood

Premieres (two versions): June 14, 1913; Ogle County, Illinois; June 13, 1914,
Lakeside, Michigan
Reviews:
Chicago Herald, June 14, 1914
Chicago Tribune, June 14, 1914
American Lumberman, June 20, 1914

"Behind the Black Cloth—"

a play in one act

by

Kenneth Sawyer Goodman—

Characters

Doctor Alessandro Blakelock
Martin Stacey
Nazel Parent   a police reporter
Vera Pope—   Blakelock's secretary.

The scene place is a room in
Doctor Blakelock's private Sanitarium
on the Connecticut shore of Long Island
Sound. It is a pleasantly furnished place
evidently used as a combination lounge
& work room by the Doctor himself—
At the back are large french windows
and to the left of them a door opening into
Blakelock's laboratory. In the right wall
is a doorway opening into the hall— there
is also a smaller door in the right wall
near the audience. There is a large table
in the center of the room with books and
magazines. At the left near the front is
a typewriter table at which Vera Pope
is typing busily —

LEAF FROM THE MS. OF *BEHIND THE BLACK CLOTH* (T41)

The Masque of Montezuma

Premiere: Mardi Gras, 1912; Art Students' League, Art Institute of Chicago
Musical setting by George A. Colburn.
Review of the publication:
New York Times, May 19, 1912

The Masque of Quetzal's Bowl

Premiere: January 6, 1911; Second Soyal [?] of the Cliff-Dwellers [Chicago]
Incidental Music by Frederick W. Root.
Hymn of the Bowl, words by Wallace Rice, music by Frederick W. Root.
A Bacchanalian Ditty, words by Wallace Rice, music by G.A. Grant-Schaefer.
Review:
Chicago Record-Herald, January 7, 1911
Special repeat performance: January 10, 1911
Review of the publication:
The New York Times, May 19, 1912

INDIVIDUAL PLAYS

At the Edge of the Wood

T10   [Published in] *The Morton Arboretum Quarterly*, 7:1 and 2, Spring &
       Summer 1971, pp9–15. "About the Masque" by Carol Doty, pp8, 16–17.

T11   Manuscript. *At the Edge of the Wood – a masque. Written for the second
       annual meeting of The Friends of Our Natural* [sic] *Landscape by K.S.
       Goodman* – [i], 19p., ink with pencil corrections, no date.

T12   Manuscript. *Masque* [10] p., ink, no date.

T13   In MQC

T14   Typescript. *At the Edge of the Wood. A Masque by K.S. Goodman.
       Written for the Second Annual Meeting of the Friends of Our Natural*
       [sic] *Landscape*. With pencil corrections in another hand [see entry T15].
       14p., no date.

T15   Typescript. *At the Edge of the Wood. A Masque by K.S. Goodman.
       Written for the Second Annual Meeting of the Friends of Our Native*

Landscape. [on cover:] *With changes by France Bendtden* [?] *Beneltden* [?] [unclear] [in the hand of KSG] 15p., no date.

T16 Typescript. *Masque.* [10] p., no date.

T17 *At the Edge of the Wood, A Masque, by K.S. Goodman.* In *The Friends of Our Native Landscape, Midsummer Booklet,* 1918. pp10-20. With an invitation by Jens Jensen.

Back of the Yards

T20 *Back of the Yards.* New York: D.C. Vaughn, 1914. [PUL]

T21 Reproduced typescript. *Stage Guild Plays. Back of the Yards by Kenneth Sawyer Goodman.* 37p., no date.

T22 Reproduced typescript. *Stage Guild Plays. Back of the Yards by Kenneth Sawyer Goodman.* 37p., no date. [This copy differs in typeface from the above]

T23 In QC-1 & 2

T24 *Back of the Yards, a realistic serious play.* In Tucker, S.M., ed. *Twelve One-act Plays for Study and Production.* Boston [c1929], pp257-282. [NYPL]

Barbara

T30 *Stage Guild Plays. Barbara, A Play in One Act By Kenneth Sawyer Goodman.* New York: Vaughn & Gomme, 1914. 32p. First edition [also X]

T31 Manuscript. *Barbara. in one act. By Kenneth Sawyer Goodman.* [32] p., ink and pencil. [The character of Archie was originally called Patmore in this version, although pencil corrections indicate the change in KSG's hand]

T32 In QC-1 & 2

Behind the Black Cloth

T40 Typescript. *Behind the Black Cloth. A Play in One Act ~~By Kenneth Sawyer Goodman~~.* [Crossed out in original] 37p., no date.

T41 Manuscript. *Behind the Black Cloth. a play in one act* by *Kenneth Sawyer Goodman−* [46] p. Ink and pencil, no date.

T42   In MQC

T43   Typescript. *Behind the Black Cloth, A Play in One Act By Kenneth Sawyer Goodman*. 37p., no date.

Caesar's Gods

T50   Cover: *Caesar's Gods. A Byzantine Masqve. By Thomas Wood Stevens and Kenneth Sawyer Goodman and Given by the Art Stvdents Leagve of Chicago Febrvary Fovr One Thovsand Nine Hvndred Thirteen*. Chicago: The Stage Guild, c1913. 27p. [One copy has an inverted binding] [also X]

T51   In MEW

The Daimio's Head

T60   *The Daimio's Head. A Masque of Old Japan. By Thomas Wood Stevens & Kenneth Sawyer Goodman. Produced by The Art Students' League, The Art Institute, Chicago, 1911*. c1911. 32p. [also X]

T61   *The Daimio's Head. A Masque of Old Japan. By Thomas Wood Stevens & Kenneth Sawyer Goodman. Produced by The Art Students' League, The Art Institute, Chicago, 1911*. Chicago: The Stage Guild, 1915. 47p. Second edition. [800 copies] [also X]

T62   In MEW

Dancing Dolls

T70   *Stage Guild Plays. Dancing Dolls By Kenneth Sawyer Goodman*. Chicago: The Stage Guild, 1915. 31p. [X]

T71   *Stage Guild Plays. Dancing Dolls By Kenneth Sawyer Goodman*. Chicago: The Stage Guild, 1923, c1915. 31p.

T72   In MQC & QC-1

T73   In Shay, Frank, ed. *Plays for Strolling Mummers*. New York: D. Appleton & Co., 1926. p[5-31] [NYPL] [PUL]

Death Watch

T80   Typescript. *The Death Watch. A Melodrama in One Act by Ben Hecht & Kenneth Sawyer Goodman*. 49p., no date. [With KSG signature and address on cover]

T81   Do. p2–49, no date.

T82   Do. [Original typescript of the above two]

Dust of the Road

T90   *Stage Guild Plays. Dust of the Road By Kenneth Sawyer Goodman.* Chicago: The Stage Guild, 1912. First edition. [NYPL] [PUL]

T91   *Stage Guild Plays. Dust of the Road By Kenneth Sawyer Goodman.* Chicago: The Stage Guild, 1947, c1912. 23p. Seventeenth edition. [also X]

T92   In QC–1 & 2

T93   In Goldstone, G.A., comp. *One-act Plays.* Boston [c1926] , pp247–265. [NYPL]

T94   In Eastman, F., comp. *Modern Religious Dramas.* New York [c1928], pp[179–] 195. [NYPL]

The Educated Anteater

T100   Manuscript. *The Educated Anteater.* Pencil, 4p., no date. Unfinished [?] .

The Egg and the Hen

T110   Typescript. *The Egg and the Hen, A Play in One-Act By Ben Hecht and Kenneth Sawyer Goodman.* [21] p. [3 copies]

T111   Typescript. *The Egg and the Hen. Hechts original draft–.* [in the hand of KSG] [27] p., with pencil corrections, no date.

T112   Manuscript. *–The Egg and the Hen.–a play in one act. by. Ben Hecht and Kenneth Sawyer Goodman.* 31p., ink, no date.

English Spy Play

T115   Manuscript. *English Spy Play.* 15p., ink with pencil corrections, no date.

Ephraim and the Winged Bear

T120   *Ephraim and the Winged Bear. A Christmas-Eve Nightmare in One Act By Kenneth Sawyer Goodman.* New York: Donald C. Vaughn, 1914. 31p. First edition. [1050 copies] [also NYPL, X]

Ephraim and the Winged Bear, Produced by Sam Hume at the Arts &Crafts Theatre, Detroit (M615)

T121 Typescript. *Ephraim and the Winged Bear. A Christmas Eve Nightmare In One Act By Kenneth Sawyer Goodman.* [29] p., no date.

T122 Manuscript. *Ephraim & The Winged Bear – a Xmas Eve Nightmare in one Act. –by–Kenneth Sawyer Goodman–.* 30p., ink and pencil, no date.

T123 In QC-1 & 2

For Old Glory

With Ben Hecht. [lost]

The Game of Chess

T140 *The Game of Chess. A Play in One Act by Kenneth Sawyer Goodman.* Chicago: The Stage Guild, 1914. [NYPL] [PUL]

T141 *The Game of Chess. A Play in One Act by Kenneth Sawyer Goodman.* Chicago: The Stage Guild, 1944, c1914. 22p. Fourth edition. [Back flap contains note on the first edition] [also X]

T142 In QC-1 & 2

T143 In Cerf, Bennett and Van H. Cartmell, ed. *Thirty Famous One-Act Plays.* New York: The Modern Library, c1943. [also X]

T144 In Gassner, John and Frederick H. Little. *Reading and Staging the Play: An Anthology of One-Act Plays.* New York: Holt, Rinehart and Winston, c1967. [also X]

T145 In Knickerbocker, E. van B., ed. *Twelve Plays.* New York [c1924], pp[259-] 276. [NYPL]

T146 In Stegner, Wallace, Edwin H. Sauer and Clarence W. Hach. *Modern Composition, Book 3* [rev. ed] New York: Holt, Rinehart and Winston, c1969, pp150-164. [also X]

T147 Reproduced typescript. *The Game of Chess by Kenneth Sawyer Goodman.* [Chicago: The Stage Guild, c1914, c1941] Tama, Iowa: no date. Edna Means Dramatic Service. [This version is an abridgement for reading purposes]

The Glorious Gateway of the West

T150 *The Glorious Gateway of the West. An Historic Pageant of the Story of Fort Wayne. Commemorating the One Hundredth Anniversary of Indiana's Admission to the Sisterhood of States. Presented in June, 1916,* *at Reservoir Park by a Company of over Eleven Hundred Citizens of Fort Wayne. The Book of the Pageant by Wallace Rice and Kenneth Sawyer Goodman. Directed by Donald Robertson.* c1916. [72] p. [also X] Includes: Fort Wayne Centennial Hymn, Music by D. Parsons Goodrich, Words by Wallace Rice; Columbia the Gem of the Ocean; The Star-Spangled Banner.

T151   Typescript. *The Glorious Gateway of the West. A Pageant for Fort Wayne By Wallace Rice and Kenneth Sawyer Goodman.* Each scene paged separately: [ii], 10p.; [i], 14p.; [iii], 14p.; [i], 10p.; [ii], 9p.; [ii], 13p. No date.

T152   Typescript. *The Glorious Gateway of the West. A Pageant for Fort Wayne. By Wallace Rice and Kenneth Sawyer Goodman.* [Includes Fort Wayne Hymn]. Each scene paged separately, pencil corrections: [iv], 6p.; [i], scene II missing; [ii], [8] p.; [i], scene IV missing; [i], 6p.; [ii], 8p. No date.

T153   Typescript. *Scene IV.* 10p., no date. With pencil corrections.

T154   Typescript. *Scene IV.* 10p., no date. [This is a copy of the above without the pencil corrections]

T155   Manuscript. *Scene IV.* 13p., ink and pencil, no date.

Goya

T160   Typescript. *Goya. by. Thomas Wood Stevens & Kenneth Sawyer Goodman.* [29] p., no date. [Cover in the hand of KSG]

T161   Typescript. [This is a copy of the above, without the cover markings by KSG]

The Green Scarf

T170   *The Stage Guild Plays No. 2. The Green Scarf. An Artificial Comedy in One Act By Kenneth Sawyer Goodman.* New York: Frank Shay [c1920]. 11p. [also NYPL, X]

T171   In MQC

The Hand of Siva

T180   Typescript. *The Hand of Siva. A melodrama in One Act By K S Goodman and Ben Hecht.* [29] p., no date.

T181   Typescript. *The Hand of Siva. A melodrama in One Act By K S Goodman and Ben Hecht.* With pencil corrections. Title on folder and pencil corrections are not in KSG's hand. Two pages are reproduced typescript.

T182   Reproduced typescript. *The Hand of Siva. A Melodrama in One Act By K.S. Goodman and Ben Hecht.* 29p.

T183   Typescript. [Folder reads:] *Goya. Copy & revise.* Typescript contains no correct identification of this as the above play. pp2-28.

T184   In WH

T185   In Shay, Frank, ed. *A Treasury of Plays for Men.* Boston, 1923. p[91-] 113. [NYPL]

T186   Manuscript. *—The Hand of Siva— —a melodrama in one act—* by *K.S. Goodman & Ben Hecht—.* [39] p., ink, no date.

Helen of Troy

T188   Manuscript. *Scenario. of Helen of Troy by Thomas Wood Stevens & Kenneth Sawyer Goodman.* Act I, 9p; Act II, [8] p; Act III, 7p. Ink and pencil, with corrections in the hand of KSG, TWS and an unidentified hand. No date.

The Hero of Santa Maria

T190   *The Stage Guild Plays No. 1. The Hero of Santa Maria. A Ridiculous Tragedy in One Act by Kenneth Sawyer Goodman and Ben Hecht.* New York: Frank Shay [c1920]. 19p. [also NYPL, X]

T191   In WH

T192   Manuscript. *—The Hero of Santa Maria— (a ridiculous tragedy in one Act) —by— Kenneth Sawyer Goodman and Ben Hecht.* 45p., ink [pencil corrections in another hand], no date.

Herring's Luck

Lost.

Holbein in Blackfriars

T210   *Holbein in Blackfriars. An Improbable Comedy by Kenneth Sawyer Goodman and Thomas Wood Stevens.* Chicago: The Stage Guild [c1913]. 32p. [also NYPL, X]

The Home Coming

T220 Typescript. *The Home Coming. A Play in One Act By Ben Hecht and Kenneth Sawyer Goodman.* 33p., with pencil corrections, no date.

T221 Typescript. *The Home Coming. A Play in One Act By Ben Hecht and Kenneth Sawyer Goodman.* 33p., no date. [A different typescript from above]

T222 Typescript. *The Home-Coming, a play in one act by Ben Hecht and Kenneth Sawyer Goodman.* [In the hand of KSG] 32p., with substantial pen and pencil corrections, no date.

An Idyll of the Shops

T230 Typescript. *An Idyll of the Shops. A Play in One Act By Ben Hecht and Kenneth Sawyer Goodman.* 22p., no date.

T231 In WH

Immigrant League

T240 Manuscript. *Immigrant Leauge* [sic] *–Pageant–* 1p., pencil, no date. Unfinished.

Julian the Apostate

See *Caesar's Gods*

The Loving Pilgrimage of Mellifonte

T250 Typescript. *The Loving Pilgrimage of Mellifonte By K Sawyer Goodman and Donald Cuyler Vaughn.* [41]p., no date.

T251 Typescript. *The Loving Pilgrimage of Mellifonte By K Sawyer Goodman and Donald Cuyler Vaughn.* [41]p., with pen corrections, no date.

T252 Do. With pencil corrections.

A Man Can Only Do His Best

T260 Reproduced typescript. *Stage Guild Plays. A Man Can Only Do His Best By Kenneth Sawyer Goodman.* 41p., no date.

T261 Typescript. *A Man Can Only Do His Best. A Farce in one act– BY– Kenneth Sawyer Goodman.* 47p., with ink corrections, no date.

T262 In QC-1 & 2

A Masque

T270   Typescript. *A Masque* [in pencil above:] *A Singer's.* . . 7p., September 1907. With pencil corrections.

T271   Typescript. *A Masque in Verse* [on cover] [Typescript is carbon copy of above] 7p., September 1907. [Without pencil corrections]

The Masque of Montezuma

T280   *The Masque of Montezuma. Thomas Wood Stevens & Kenneth Sawyer Goodman.* Chicago: The Stage Guild [c1912]. unpaged. [iv, 26p.] [also X]

T281   In MEW

The Masque of Quetzal's Bowl

T290   *The Masque of Quetzal's Bowl. Written for the Second Anniversary of the House Warming of the Cliff-Dwellers by Thomas Wood Stevens and Kenneth Sawyer Goodman.* No publisher, no date. [This is a published edition. There are several copies. One has an inverted binding.] [also X]

T291   In MEW

A Masque of Summer

T300   Manuscript. *A Masque of Summer.* 5[3 remaining]p., pencil, no date. Unfinished.

A Pageant for Independence Day

T310   *A Pageant for Independence Day by Kenneth Sawyer Goodman & Thomas Wood Stevens, authors of.* . . Chicago: The Stage Guild [c1912]. unpaged. [vi, 31p.] [also NYPL, X]

T311   In MEW

The Parting

T320   Cover: *The Parting. a melodrama in one act. by K. S. Goodman – 707 Railway Exchange Chicago, Ills.*

T321   Typescript. *The Parting. A Melodrama in One Act By Kenneth Sawyer*

~~Goodman~~. [Crossed out in original] 29p., with pencil corrections, no date.

T322   In MQC

The Passing of the Torch

T330   Typescript. *The Passing of the Torch by Paul Hervieux. Translated by Kenneth Sawyer Goodman.* Each act paged separately: 30p., 20p., 25p., 17p. No date.

T331   Typescript. *The Torch. Le Course du Flambeau. A Play in Four Acts by Paul Herrieux* [sic] . *Translated by Kenneth Sawyer Goodman.* Each act paged separately: [20] p., 16p., 28p., 11p. No date.

T332   Manuscript. *The Torch. Le Course du Flambeau. A play in four acts by Paul Hervieux. Translated by Kenneth Sawyer Goodman.* 141p., ink and pencil, no date.

T333   Typescript. [Parts of Act I, III and IV. Act I, pp25-32; Act III, pp1-25; Act IV, p8. With ink corrections]

The Poem of David

T340   Typescript. *The Poem of David.* 26p., no date.

T341   Typescript. *The Poem of David.* 41p., no date. [With extensive ink corrections in an unknown hand]

T342   Manuscript. *The Poem of David. –a play in One Act* [hand of KSG] *by K S Goodman and Ben Hecht* [another hand] . 44p., ink and pencil, no date.

T343   Typescript. *The Poem of David. A Play in One Act By* [hand of KSG] *Kenneth Sawyer Goodman & Ben Hecht.* 35p., no date. [With minor ink corrections. On cover label, in pencil, *Original ending* (not included)]

The Prince of Pavonia

T350   Manuscript. *The Prince of Pavonia. A play in two acts.* 24p., ink, no date.

Queens Tragedy

T360   Manuscript. *Queens Tragedy.* [Title on cover only] 15[21] p., ink and pencil, no date.

Rainald and the Red Wolf

T370 *Rainald and the Red Wolf, being a masque of the pilgrims and the towns-folk of Lavayne, and how they played their shrove tide miracle before the* Lord Waldemar. As written by Kenneth Sawyer Goodman and Thomas Wood Stevens, for the annual Mardi Gras Festival of the Art Students' League, Chicago, 1914.* [c1914] , 34p. [also X]

T371 Typescript. *A Mediaeval Masque. Written for production by the Art Students' League of the Art Institute of Chicago, Mardi Gras, February 24, 1914, by Kenneth Sawyer Goodman and Thomas Wood Stevens. Music for the Masque by* [there is a blank space here] . The typescript is on the stationery of Thomas Wood Stevens. The manuscript is in ink with ink and pencil corrections in the hand of KSG. Two opening pages are marked *Scenario (a medieval masque) − 12th Century −*, in pencil in the hand of KSG. 31p., no date.

T372 In MEW

The Red Flag

T380 Typescript. *The Red Flag. A Comedy in One Act by Kenneth Sawyer Goodman.* 35p., no date.

T381 Typescript. *The Red Flag. A Comedy in One Act by ~~Kenneth Sawyer Goodman~~.* [Crossed out in original] 35p., no date. With pencil corrections.

T382 Manuscript. *The Red Flag. A Comedy in One Act − by Kenneth Sawyer Goodman.* [40] p., no date. Ink and pencil, with one page of typescript.

T383 In MQC

A Revision of Salome

T390 *A Revision of Salome, or, Why Young Men Leave Home. A Refined Opera in One Convulsion. Book by Kenneth Goodman and Murray Nelson. Lyrics by Angus Hibbard.* 8[16?] p., no publisher, no date. [Half of the pages are blank, although the text is complete. It is unclear whether this is a proof sheet or an unusual design idea]

Ryland

T400 *Ryland, a comedy* [by] Thomas Wood Stevens & Kenneth Sawyer Goodman. Chicago: The Stage Guild [c1912] . 29p. [prompt-book] [NYPL]

T401 In Mayorga, Margaret Gardner. *Representative One-Act Plays by American Authors.* Boston: Little, Brown and Company, 1919. [also X]

Saybrook

T410 Manuscript. *Saybrook. Creole Play.* 4p., pencil, no date. Unfinished.

Scout Play

T415 Manuscript. *Scout Play.* 26p., ink with pencil corrections, no date.

A Short Melodrama for Vaudeville

T420 Typescript. *A Short Melodrama for Vaudeville By Kenneth Sawyer Goodman. All rights reserved.* 24p., no date.

T421 Manuscript. *A —Short melodrama— for Vaudeville By Kenneth Sawyer Goodman. all rights reserved.* 24p., no date. [Cover marked "for C.D."]

The Stove

T430 Manuscript. *The Stove.* 10p., pencil, no date. [In verse]

To Vote or Not To Vote

T440 Manuscript. *To Vote or not to Vote (a play for amateurs).* 4p., pencil, no date. Unfinished.

The Toy Maker

T450 Typescript. *The Toy Maker. A Melodrama in Three Acts by Kenneth Sawyer Goodman.* 51p., no date. [This copy contains only Act I] [Three copies]

T451 Manuscript. *Outline and Fragments from The Toy Maker a play.* Ink and pencil. [Various pages and styles of paper, some loose, some pinned together]

The Two Lamps

T456 In WH

T457 Proof sheets. *The Two Lamps, A Melodrama.* No publisher, no date. [Probably from The Wonder Hat] pp43-[79].

T458   Manuscript. *The Two Lamps. a melodrama in one Act. by— Ben Hecht and Kenneth Sawyer Goodman.* 43p., ink, no date.

T459   Typescript. *The Two Lamps, A Melodrama in One Act by Ben Hecht and Kenneth Sawyer Goodman.* 36p., no date.

Untitled No. 1

T460   Manuscript. A Play in One Act.
Characters: A Prussian General, A Prussian Captain, A Prussian Lieutenant, An orderly, A private soldier, A Sergeant, Two Infantrymen, [A Colonel]. [15] p., ink and pencil, no date. Unfinished.

Untitled No. 2

T470   Manuscript. A Play in Two Acts.
Characters: Mrs. Bardish, Letty, Dr. Murdoch, Dr. Ware, Alexandra, Gus, Peter, Mrs. L., Landy. Act I [23p.], Act II (unfinished) [5] p., ink.

Untitled No. 3

T480   Manuscript. Sketch.
Characters: The Bishop, Slade. [5] p., pencil, no date.

Untitled No. 4

T490   Manuscript. Characters: Mrs. Quentin Annersly, Quentin Annersly, Mrs. Bently Prentice, Wade McCullough, Bently Prentice, Miller, Mrs. Annersly's butler. 11p., pencil, no date. Unfinished.

Untitled No. 5

T500   Manuscript. Characters: Asa Doane, Truth Doane, Jed Doane. 4p., pencil, no date. Unfinished.

Untitled No. 6

T510   Manuscript. Characters: Mrs. S., Mrs. M., Lucile, Mr. S. 17p., pencil, no date. Unfinished. [With a synopsis of the play in the hand of Mrs. Goodman, summarizing 13 scenes] 11p., pencil, no date.

Untitled No. 7

T515   Typescript. Characters: Pierrot, The Minister of Police, The Secretary, First Police Agent, Second Police Agent, A Clerk, A Footman. 13p., no date.

Untitled No. 8

T517   Manuscript. *Act IV – Foss's law office.*
Characters: Foss, Pierce, Wilkinson, Tinblatter, Hines, The Boss, et al. 2p., no date.

Wine of Luck

T520   Cover: *Wine of Luck*
Manuscript: *(Garden Play)*
Typescript: *(Garden Play.)*
Unpaged, ink, pencil and typing, with corrections. [Various sizes and styles of paper]

The Wonder Hat

T530   *Stage Guild Plays. The Wonder Hat.* [cover only:] *A Harlequinade in One Act by Kenneth Sawyer Goodman and Ben Hecht.* Chicago: The Stage Guild, 1923 [1925?] [c1916, 1920, 1923, 1925] [also NYPL, c1920]

T531   *The Wonder Hat, by Kenneth Sawyer Goodman and Ben Hecht.* Chicago: The Stage Guild, 1923 [1925?]. 32p. Prompt-book. [NYPL]

T532   *The Wonder Hat, by Kenneth Sawyer Goodman and Ben Hecht.* Chicago: The Stage Guild, 1946. 32p. [also X]

T533   Manuscript. *The Wonder Hat. A Harlequinade. –in one scene– –by– Ben Hecht and Kenneth Sawyer Goodman.* 47p., no date. [Entirely in the hand of KSG]

T534   In WH

T535   In Mayorga, Margaret Gardner. *Representative One-Act Plays by American Authors.* Boston: Little, Brown and Company, 1919. [also X]

T536   Typescript. *The Wonder Hat, A Harlequinade in One Scene By Kenneth Sawyer Goodman.* 39p., no date.

T537   Typescript. *The Wonder Hat* [in the hand of KSG on cover]. Divided into: "Prologue" and "The Act." [Be]*n Hechts* [original dra]*ft* on cover.

COLLECTIONS

The Daimio's Head and Other Masques

T538   by Kenneth Sawyer Goodman and Thomas Wood Stevens.

Chicago: The Stage Guild, c.1912. [also X]

Includes: *The Daimio's Head. The Masque of Montezuma. The Masque of Quetzal's Bowl.*

Quick Curtains–1

T540   Chicago: The Stage Guild, 1915.
First Edition. Various pp.

This volume contains individual first editions of the plays bound in one.

Includes: *Dust of the Road. The Game of Chess. Barbara. Ephraim and the Winged Bear. Back of the Yards. Dancing Dolls. A Man Can Only Do His Best.*

Printed by The Lancaster Printing Company, Lancaster, Pa.

From *Quick Curtains*:

Dust of the Road was first produced by the Wisconsin Dramatic Society at the Fuller Opera House, Madison, Wisconsin, in January, 1913, with the following caste [sic]:

Peter Steele . . . . .H.G. Abendroth
Prudence . . . . Ada Briggs
An Old Man . . . . M.E. Spear
The Tramp. . . . . .Thomas Wood Stevens

The Game of Chess was first produced by B. Iden Payne under the auspices of the Chicago Theatre Society at the Fine Arts Theatre, November 18th, 1913, with the following caste [sic]:

Alexis Alexandrovitch . . . . Walter Hampden
Boris Ivanovitch Shamrayeff . . . . .Whitford Kane
Constantine . . . . T.W. Gibson
Footman . . . . .Howard Plinge

THE WONDER HAT, PRODUCED BY SAM HUME AT THE
ARTS & CRAFTS THEATRE, DETROIT (M630)

Barbara was first produced under the direction of Mr. B. Iden Payne at the Fine Arts Theatre, Chicago, December 9th, 1913, with the following caste [sic] :

Barbara . . . . Miss Mona Limerick
Archie. Mr. Dallas Anderson
Eccles (Archie's manservant) . . . . .Mr. B. Iden Payne

"This first edition of *Barbara*, printed . . . in March, 1914, for VAUGHAN & GOMME, New York, consists of one thousand and fifty copies on laid paper."

Ephraim and the Winged Bear. A Christmas Eve Nightmare in One Act. (title page)
New York: Donald C. Vaughan, 1914.
"This first edition of *Ephraim and the Winged Bear,* printed . . . in December, 1914, for DONALD C. VAUGHAN, New York, consists of one thousand and fifty copies on laid paper."

Back of the Yards. A Play in One Act. (title page)
New York: Donald C. Vaughan, 1914.

Dancing Dolls was first produced by the Department of Dramatic Arts of the Carnegie Institute of Technology, at Pittsburgh, June 15, 1914, under the direction of Mr. Thomas Wood Stevens, with the following caste [sic] :

IN THE PROLOGUE

Fleurette . . . . Doris Williams
Colinette . . . . Alice S. Guthrie
Blanche. . . . . Inez M. Krebs
A Dancer . . . . Elizabeth Duffy

IN THE PLAY

Gilles . . . . .Charles F. Steen
Buffo . . . . .Leo Beiter
Mezzetin . . . . Charles Meredith
Margot . . . . Betty Brown
Finetta . . . . Marcella Frederick
Clementina. .Florence Little
The Notary . . . . Charles H. Duffy

A Man Can Only Do His Best was first produced under the direction of

44

Mr. B. Iden Payne at The Gaiety Theatre, Manchester, England, July 6, 1914, with the following caste [sic] :

Gilles, A Mountebank. . . . . Wallace Evennett
Doctor Funustasius Labulgobulus,
A Quack . . . . Christian Morrow
Captain Pasuli, A Highwayman. . . . . Ernest C. Cassel
The Mayor. . . . . .William Dexter
A Gendarme. Ronan Sweeney
Another Gendarme . . . . Norman Walker
Simonetta, The Mayor's Wife. . . . . Edith Smith
Julietta, The Keeper of a Lodging House . . . .Frances Waring

"This first edition of *A Man Can Only Do His Best,* printed . . . in February, 1915, for THE STAGE GUILD, Chicago, consists of nine hundred copies on laid paper."

Quick Curtains-2

T541   Chicago: The Stage Guild, 1923.
Second Edition. 178pp. [also NYPL, X]

Note by Thomas Wood Stevens

Includes: *Dust of the Road. The Game of Chess. Barbara. Ephraim and the Winged Bear. Back of the Yards. A Man Can Only Do His Best.*

Printed by The Eddy Press Corporation, Pittsburgh, Pa.

From *Quick Curtains*:

Dust of the Road was first produced by the Wisconsin Dramatic Society at the Fuller Opera House, Madison, Wisconsin, in January, 1913, with the following cast:

Peter Steele . . . . .H.G. Abendroth
Prudence Steele. Ada Briggs
An Old Man . . . . M.E. Spear
The Tramp. . . . . .Thomas Wood Stevens

The Game of Chess was first produced by B. Iden Payne under the auspices of the Chicago Theatre Society at the Fine Arts Theatre, November 18th, 1913, with the following cast:

Alexis Alexandrovitch . . . . Walter Hampden
Boris Ivanovitch Shamrayeff . . . . .Whitford Kane

Constantine . . . . T.W. Gibson
Footman . . . . Howard Plinge

Barbara was first produced under the direction of Mr. B. Iden Payne at the Fine Arts Theatre, Chicago, December 9th, 1913, with the following cast:

Barbara . . . . Miss Mona Limerick
Archie. . . . . Mr. Dallas Anderson
Eccles (Archie's man-servant). . . . . .Mr. B. Iden Payne

Ephraim and the Winged Bear was first produced at the Arts and Crafts Theater, Detroit, December, 1916, under the direction of Sam Hume, with the following cast:

Ephraim Bumsteeple . . . . .C.E. Hilton
Bertha, his wife. . . . . Eva W. Victor
A Maid . . . . Marian McMichael
Edward Sheets . . . . .A.L. Weeks
A Young Woman, from the streets . . . . . . Lento Fulwell
A Young Man, in a silk hat . . . . .Samuel L. Breck

Back of the Yards was first performed at Hull House Theatre; also at the Arts Theatre, Carnegie Institute of Technology, Pittsburgh, under the direction of Mr. Chester W. Wallace, with the following cast:

A Priest. . . . . Howard Forman Smith
A Police Sergeant . . . . .Barry Buchanan
A Boy. . . . . Kenneth Thomson
The Boy's Mother . . . . .Anna Dice
A Girl . . . . Sara Floyd

A Man Can Only Do His Best was first produced under the direction of Mr. B. Iden Payne at the Gaiety Theatre, Manchester, England, July 6, 1914, with the following cast:

Gilles, A Mountebank. . . . . Wallace Evennett
Doctor Funustasius Labulgobulus,
A Quack . . . . .Christian Morrow
Captain Pasuli, A Highwayman. . . . . .Ernest C. Cassel
The Mayor. . . . . .William Dexter
A Gendarme. .Ronan Sweeney
Another Gendarme . . . . Norman Walker
Simonetta, The Mayor's Wife. . . . . Edith Smith
Julietta, The Keeper of a Lodging House . . . .Frances Waring

Quick Curtains and More Quick Curtains

T545 No title page. Various pp.
This volume contains individual editions of the plays bound in one by Marjorie Sawyer Goodman Graff. [X]

Includes: *Dust of the Road. Back of the Yards. The Game of Chess. Barbara. Ephraim and the Winged Bear. A Man Can Only Do His Best. More Quick Curtains.*

Printed by The Lancaster Printing Company, Lancaster, Pa.

From *Quick Curtains and More Quick Curtains:*

Dust of the Road. Chicago: The Stage Guild, 1923. Fourth edition.

Back of the Yards. A Play in One Act. New York: Donald C. Vaughan, 1914.
"This first edition of *Back of the Yards*, printed. . .in December, 1914, for DONALD C. VAUGHAN, New York, consists of one thousand and fifty copies on laid paper."

The Game of Chess. A Play in One Act. Chicago: The Stage Guild, 1926. Second edition.
"This first edition [sic] of *The Game of Chess*, printed . . . in April, 1914, for VAUGHAN & GOMME, New York, consists of one hundred and fifty copies on Japanese Vellum." [This edition is not on Japanese Vellum and is marked "The Libby Company Printers, Chicago, Illinois" on the bottom of the same page]

Barbara. A Play in One Act. New York: Vaughan & Gomme, 1914.
"This first edition of *Barbara*, printed . . . in March, 1914, for VAUGHAN & GOMME, New York, consists of one thousand and fifty copies on laid paper."

Ephraim and the Winged Bear. A Christmas-Eve Nightmare in One Act. New York: Donald C. Vaughan, 1914. [Inside cover: Ex-Libris The Chicago Little Theatre]
"This first edition of *Ephraim and the Winged Bear*, printed . . . in December, 1914, for DONALD C. VAUGHAN, New York, consists of one thousand and fifty copies on laid paper."

A Man Can Only Do His Best. A Fantastic Comedy in One Act. Chicago: The Stage Guild, 1915.
"This first edition of *A Man Can Only Do His Best*, printed . . . in Feb-

ruary, 1915, for THE STAGE GUILD, Chicago, consists of nine hundred copies on laid paper."

More Quick Curtains. [Contains same material and pagination as 1923 edition of *More Quick Curtains* (T550)]

Quick Curtains and More Quick Curtains

T546   Another copy bound by Cuneo. Each play retains the original cover. [X]

More Quick Curtains

T550   Chicago: The Stage Guild, 1923. 159pp. [also X]

Note by B. Iden Payne.

Includes: *The Green Scarf. The Red Flag. The Parting. Behind the Black Cloth. At the Edge of the Wood. Dancing Dolls.*

Printed by the Eddy Press Corporation, Pittsburgh, Pa.

From *More Quick Curtains:*

The Green Scarf. Copyright, 1920, by Frank Shay. (title page)

The Green Scarf was originally produced by the Guild Players, Pittsburgh, February 21, 1920, with the following cast:

A Man. . . . . C. Frederick Steen
A Woman. . . . . Hazel Beck

The Red Flag. A Comedy in One Act. (title page)

The Red Flag was first produced by The Player's Workshop, Chicago, July 19, 1916, under the direction of Clarence Thomas, with the following cast:

Collin Weyland . . . . E. Roslyn Kirkbride
Marna Swanbridge, his sister-in-law . . . . .Helen Cook
Jack Martin .Edward Balzerit
Antoinette, an elderly lady's maid . . . . . . .Margaret Allen
Prost, Collin Weyland's man-servant . . . . .Donovan Yuell
The Reverend Comingo Bird . . . . Clarence Thomas

The Parting. A Melodrama. (title page)

The Parting was first produced at the Theater of the Carnegie Institute

48

of Technology, under the direction of B. Iden Payne, with the following cast:

Max, A Prussian Spy . . . . James Church
Pere Rigaude, A Concierge . . . . .Howard McClenahan
Henri Fautrelle, A Lame Cobbler . . . . . .David S. Gaither
Gabrielle, A Young French Actress . . . . Alma Lind

Behind the Black Cloth. A Melodrama in One Act. (title page)

Behind the Black Cloth was produced in February, 1923, by the Guild Players of Pittsburgh, under the direction of Theodore Viehman, with the following cast:

Doctor Alessandro Blakelock . . . . .Theodore Viehman
Martin Stacey . . . . .Phillip R. Thorn
Nagel Parent, A Police Reporter . . . . John A. Willard
Vera Pope, Blakelock's Secretary . . . . Sara Floyd

At the Edge of the Wood. (no title page)

At the Edge of the Wood was originally produced by "The Friends of Our Native Landscape" in 1918, and has been repeated annually by the same organization.

CHARACTERS

A Faun	An Architect
A Wood Sprite	A Merchant
A Poet	A Working Man
An Artist	A Working Woman

Dancing Dolls. (no title page)

Dancing Dolls was first produced by the Department of Drama of the Carnegie Institute of Technology, at Pittsburgh, June 15, 1914, under the direction of Mr. Thomas Wood Stevens, with the following cast:

Gilles . . . . .Charles F. Steen
Buffo . . . . .Leo Beiter
Mezzetin . . . . Charles Meredith
Margot . . . . .Betty Weston
Finetta . . . . Marcella Frederick
Clementina . . . . .Florence Little
The Notary . . . . Charles H. Duffy

Masques of East & West

T560   by Thomas Wood Stevens & Kenneth Sawyer Goodman. Edited by Wallace Rice with a Foreword by Percy MacKaye.

New York: Vaughan & Gomme, 1914. [also X]

Includes: *The Daimio's Head. The Masque of Montezuma. Caesar's Gods. Rainald and the Red Wolf. A Pageant for Independence Day. The Masque of Quetzal's Bowl.*

The Daimio's Head was first produced by the Art Students' League at the Art Institute, Chicago, Mardi-Gras, 1911, with the following caste [sic]:

Buchi, A Badger-Man, a good goblin . . . . Richard Babcock
Kobayashi   . . . gentlemen tea drinkers. . .   Frank McNellis
Shimidzu   Robert Hertzberg
Uta   . . . . dancing girls . . . .   Elsie Braunhold
Yasu   Ana Heller
Funakoshi, a young Samurai . . . . . .Thomas Wood Stevens
O Toyo San, a Princess . . . . .Edith Emerson
Asano   Counsellors of the Daimio   Allen E. Philbrick
Oishi   . . . .   of Sendai   . . . .   Gerrit Sinclair
Matsudaira Mutsa No Kami,
     Daimio of Sendai . . . . E. Roslyn Kirkbride
A Fox-Woman, a wicked goblin . . . . . . .Luvena Buchanan
Hokusai, an artist . . . . .Frederick Cowley
His Pupil . . . . Milton Newman
A Magistrate . . . . Ralph Holmes
First Priest   at the Temple   Roy Hambleton
Second Priest   . . . . .   of Kitoji   . . . . . .   Carl Scheffler
The Abbot of the Temple . . . . .Frederick Cowley
A Dancer . . . . Mrs. Michitaro Ogawa

The Masque of Montezuma was written for, and first produced by, the Art Students' League, at the Art Institute, Chicago, February 20, 1912. The original musical setting was written by George A. Colburn. The setting for the production was designed by Allen E. Philbrick and A.N. Rebori, and painted under their direction. The caste [sic] was as follows:

Huitzil, the War-God . . . . .Thomas Wood Stevens
High Priest of Huitzil . . . . .Frederick K. Cowley
Second Priest of Huitzil . . . . .Roy Tyrrell
Cuitlahautzin, Montezuma's Brother . . . . . Frank McNellis

Guatomotzin, nephew to Montezuma . . . . Roy Hambleton
Montezuma . . . . E. Roslyn Kirkbride
The Eldest Chief . . . . Gerrit Sinclair
High Priest of Quetzal . . . . Francis Samms
First Priestess of Quetzal. . . . . Elaine Wyman
Second Priestess of Quetzal . . . . Florence Levy
A Messenger . . . . Harry L. Gage
Montezuma's Envoy. . . . . Milton Newman
An Aztec Warrior . . . . Charles Mullen
First Aztec Woman . . . . Luvena Buchanan
Second Aztec Woman. . . . . Frances Thorp
Cortez. . . . . D.M. Stebbins
Marina, Interpreter for Cortez . . . . Nouart Seron
Alvarado . . . . E.M. Sincere
Padre Olmedo. . . . . A.D. Gibbs
Bernal Diaz . . . . C.D. Faulkner

Groups representing Montezuma's court, the priests and priestesses of the Aztec gods, singers, dancers, artificers, Aztec warriors following Cuitlahautzin, Spaniards and Tlascalans following Cortez

Caesar's Gods was written for and first produced by the Art Students' League at the Art Institute, Chicago, Mardi-Gras 1913. The musical setting was written by George A. Colburn. The caste [sic] was as follows:

Julian, Emperor of the East. . . . . H.C. Kiefer
Libianus, the Quaestor . . . . T.W. Stevens
The Priest of Mithras . . . . K.S. Goodman
The Patriarch of Constantinople. . . . . E. Roslyn Kirkbride
The Bishop of Edessa . . . . Jacob Bischof
The Count of the Sacred Largess . . . . H.C. Stanley
The Praefect of the Bed Chamber . . . . Alan Swisher
Attirius, a young Pagan noble,
    nephew to Libianus . . . . Lance Hart
Tigillinus, an old Pagan,
    friend to Attirius . . . . E.J. Zillmer
Chion, a Greek philosopher . . . . Gerrit Sinclair
Anactoria, a Pagan courtesan . . . . Elaine Hyman
A Dancer. . . . . Margaret Dixon
A Persian Envoy . . . . Milton Newman

51

An Armenian Envoy . . . . .Edward Vysekal
An Acolyte of Mithras . . . . .Luvena Buchanan

A Group representing Apollo and the Muses
A Group representing Dionysus and Bacchantes
A Group representing Artemis and Nymphs
A Group representing Athene and her Votaries

Acolytes of Mithras, Monks, Hand-maidens, Trumpeters, Palace Guards, Bishops, Courtiers, Soldiers, Attendants of the Envoys

Rainald and the Red Wolf was first produced by the Art Students' League, at the Art Institute, Chicago, Mardi-Gras, 1914, with musical setting by Frederick Hart, scenery by Gerrit Sinclair, and with the following caste [sic] :

OF LAVAYNE

Rainald, Count of Lavayne . . . . .Lance Wood Hart
Ysobel, His wife, Countess of Lavayne. . . . Blanche Dalton
Florino, Equerry to the Countess . . . . E. Roslyn Kirkbride
The Bishop of Lavayne. . . . . .Raymond Mammes
The Crier of Lavayne . . . . George Shepherd
The Guild-Master of the Armorers . . . . . L. James Merwin
The Guild-Master of the
    Wool Merchants. . . . . .Charles E. Mullin
The Guild-Master of the Bakers . . . . Roy H. Shinew
First Burgher's Wife. . . . . Catherine Rolff
Second Burgher's Wife . . . . .Beatrice Sherman
Third Burgher's Wife . . . . .Sarah Hoover
An Old Woman. . . . . .Luvena Buchanan

Citizens of Lavayne, Ladies in Waiting, Courtiers, etc.

OF THE BLACK COMPANY

Waldemar, Baron of Ludoc
    and Degramour . . . . Henry C. Kiefer
His Captain . . . . Elmer Wolf
His Herald . . . . Emil G. Zillmer

Comrades of the Black Company

Of the Brotherhood of Pilgrims

The Crier of the Pilgrims. . . . . Nils Wikstrom
An Old Gleeman .Fred Kuehn
A Jongleur. . . . . .Louis Klebba

In the Miracle Play

A Lady, Representing the City. . . . .Frances Avelina Thorpe
Fear . . . . William Owen
Greed . . . . . . Her Counselors . . . . . .Bernard Armstrong
Sloth. . . . . Erving Kraut
Church . . . . Donald Ordway
An Angel. . . . . Elsinore Girton
A Wolf . . . . .Ralph Sieweke
A Crusader. Lance Wood Hart

The time is the Twelfth Century.

A Pageant for Independence Day was written at the suggestion of the Sane Fourth Association of Chicago, and first produced under its auspices, assisted by the Chicago Woman's Club, at Jackson Park, Chicago, the evening of July 4, 1911 . . . Scene I. was played by students of the Art Institute under the direction of Mr. Stevens and Mr. Cowley. Scene II. was played by members of Mr. Donald Robertson's class in the Cosmopolitan School of Music and Dramatic Art. Scene III. was played by the Players' Club of the Young Men's Hebrew Institute under the direction of Lester Alden. Scene IV. was played by members of The Palette and Chisel Club assisted by Mr. Langan and Mr. Owen. Caste [sic]:

The Town Crier. . . . . William Owen

Scene I.

A Lame Boy. Oliver Rainville
Paul Revere . . . . Charles Herbert
Dick, one of the Sons of Liberty . . . . Ward Thornton
Mr. Wentworth, a Merchant. . . . . .B.L. Matthews
Mistress Truth Jackson . . . . .Bess Devine
Colonel Spotswood, a British Officer. . . . . . Frank Herbert
William Jackson, a Loyalist Merchant . . . . J.H. McFarland
Governor Hutchinson. . . . . J.P. York
Ensign Pritchard . . . . Edward Cristman
Samuel Adams . . . . .Frederick Cowley

SCENE II.

Martha Washington . . . . Gladys Tilden
Miss Malby. . . . . .Jane Heap
Mrs. Fairfax . . . . .Sarah Mann
Lady Caroline Dunmore . . . . .Olive Garnett
Colonel George Washington. . . . . Thomas Langan
Edmund Pendelton . . . . .R.B. Nelson
Patrick Henry . . . . .Frank Hardin
Charles Dunmore. . . . . Rosco Brink
Pompey. . . . . .E. Griffith

SCENE III.

Captain Parker, of the
    Lexington Minute Men . . . . Bernard Friedman
Mr. Harrington . . . . .Henry Boyell
A Young Farmer . . . . N.R. Pastel
Bowman, a patriot messenger. . . . . S. Harrison
Major Pitcairn. . . . . J. Lewis Baskin
Lord Percy. .Herman Schover
Lieutenant Nash . . . . Phillip H. Goldstein
A Trooper . . . . .D. Levin
Mrs. Harrington. . . . . Miss Rosenberg

SCENE IV.

First Sentry . . . . .O.E. Hake
Second Sentry . . . . .Martin Hennings
The Butcher's Boy. . . . . George Baer
Lieutenant Prosby . . . . Carl Scheffler
General Sullivan . . . . .Theodore Lely
General Washington. . . . . Thomas Langan
Colonel Wells . . . . George Seidendeck
Captain Marsh of the Militia . . . . Karl Krafft
Colonel Reed . . . . .Ezra Winter
Colonel Patterson, British Army. . . . . .Harry Engle
The Messenger . . . . William Owen

The Masque of Quetzal's Bowl was written for the second anniversay of
the House Warming of the Cliff-Dwellers, February 10, 1911, and produced by Donald Robertson with scenery by Allen E. Philbrick with
the following caste [sic] :

IN THE WORK-SHOP

An Artificer . . . . .Hart Conway
An Antiquarian. . . . . Donald Robertson

. IN THE VISION

Cocijo-Eza, the old King . . . . .Robert R. Jarvie
Cocijo-Pij, the Young King . . . . .K.S. Goodman
Uija-Tao, High Priest of Mitla. . . . . .Thomas Wood Stevens
An Aztec Councilor . . . . Charles E. Nixon
A Copa . . . . .Allen E. Philbrick

Scene I. An Artificer's Work-Shop
Scene II. The Artificer's Vision—A Temple at Mitla
Scene III. The Work-Shop

The Wonder Hat and Other One Act Plays

T570 by Kenneth Sawyer Goodman and Ben Hecht.

New York: D. Appleton and Company, 1925. [also NYPL, X]

Prefatory note by Thomas Wood Stevens.

Includes: *The Wonder Hat. The Two Lamps. An Idyll of the Shops. The Hand of Siva. The Hero of Santa Maria.*

From *The Wonder Hat and Other One Act Plays:*

The Wonder Hat was originally produced at the Arts and Crafts Theatre, Detroit, Michigan in 1916. Set designed by Sam Hume. Notice: The text of "The Wonder Hat" as given in this edition represents the final revision of the play by the authors.
The Hero of Santa Maria was originally presented by the Washington Square Players, at the Comedy Theater, New York, on the night of February 12, 1917.

EARLY DRAWING OF MAN SMOKING [X]

POEMS

DESCRIPTIVE KEY AND COLLECTIONS

CODE *Title (Alternate Title by Wallace Rice)* Date
First line of text
Format of available copies Collection(s)*

*The following are the keyed collections:

1.
"Various verses from those done 1908-1909,
Finished and revised
April. 1910.
including
Some of the songs set to music
by Mrs Giddens [?] ."

2.
"A Cycle of Ballades"

3.
"Verses finnished [sic] prior to 1907
Verses laid out April 1910 as not to be
included in later selections—
Including
the present [?] of the college verse"

4.

[A group of poems clasped together]

5.

"April 1910.
  Shorter verse done after leaving
Princeton & prior to Dec 1907—
  These include several ballades
and The Cloud [?] Cycle Songs also some
  others set to music by Mrs Giddes [?]."

6.

[A large typed and indexed collection, done on KSG's machine]

7.

A Riven Lute. Poems and Songs by Kenneth Sawyer Goodman. With an introduction by Henry Van Dyke [not present in the dummy]. Edited, with a Memoir [also not present], by Wallace Rice. Chicago, The Brothers of the Book, 1919. [This was prepared for publication, but remains in dummy form. Two pages of typeset were later prepared. See earlier expanded comments.] [also X]

DRAWING OF A CAT AND A BEAR (M35)

INDIVIDUAL POEMS

P70 *At Carnival Time*
      Say thou hast thought of me when the mad dance
P71   *Nassau Lit* 61:9 p389

P80 *At the Theatre*   September 1909
      A man beside me quotes the closing price
      Dummy   7

P90 *Autumn (Autumn Parting)*
      We stood my love and I at the days end
P91   Manuscript, ink and typescript   also 3, 7

      Autumn Noon
      see *A Rhymer's Summer*

      Autumn Parting
      see *Autumn*

      Autumn Perishes
      see *Ballade*

P100 *Autumn Song*   December 1907
      Wind in the standing rye
      Dummy   7

P110 *Autumn Song (Another Year)*   September 1906
      Sweet! Though the summer hath blown over
P111 Manuscript, ink and typescript   also 3, 7

P120 *Autumn Song (The Call of Autumn)*
      Somewhere beyond the hills
      Typescript   also 7
P121 *Nassau Lit* 61:4 p131

P130 *Autumn Wandering*
      I'm bound no [sic?] whither; I do but follow
      Dummy   7

P140 *The Avalanche*   January 1901
      Swifter than snow from the mountains
      Typescript   also 6

P150 *The Ballad of the Pool Room*   March 1901
      Last night when out across the snow
      Typescript   also 6
      [No **P160** or **P170**]

P329	*Ballade (All for Love)* from *A Cycle of Ballades* Ships at sea in a southern gale Typescript	2, also 5, 7
P326	*Ballade (Autumn Perishes)* from *A Cycle of Ballades* Great winds that run aloft from star to star Manuscript, ink and typescript	October 1906 2, also 5, 7
P325	*Ballade (Ultimate)* from *A Cycle of Ballades* If wings being weary with too soft a nest Manuscript, ink and typescript	October 1906 2, also 5, 7
P180	*The Ballade of Jesses* [?] *Suitors* Manuscript, pencil, 2p., no date.	
	Because of You see *Songs*	
P190	*Below the Spanish Steps* Below the Spanish steps a house four walls Typescript with ink corrections	March 1907 also 7
P200	*Between Dark and Day* Between dark and day Dummy	7
	Bright Lips, Light Heart see *Song*	
P210	*Butte des Morts* I'm dreaming of the ripples Typescript Pub: *The Daily Northwestern,* March 21, 1903	1902 also 6
P220	*The Cafe Violinist* With graceful sweep of immelodious bow Dummy	November 1910 7
	The Call of Autumn see *Autumn Song*	
P230	*A Cavalier Song* These are thy ashes, oh! dream that has fled	May 1903

Manuscript, pencil with pencil corrections,
typescript   also 6, 7

P240   *Celestial Golf*
When our last great match is finished
Dummy   7

P250   *The Chains of Memory*   Februàry 1901
Do we dream, or when we slumber
Typescript   also 6

P260   *The Church Yard*
These pious Dead, when living, said to me
Typescript   also 7

P270   *Circe*
She pours, for them that drink with her, a chalice
Typescript, with pencil corrections in
another hand   also 7

P280   *Class Poem (Days Reverberant)*   June 1906
Things beautiful may vanish from sight
Typescript   also 7
P281   *Princeton University Class Book* 1906 pp26–27 [PUL]

P290   *Columbine*   September 1909
What know I of Columbine?
Dummy   7

P300   *Compensations*   November 1905
Treasures that quicken and lure
Dummy   7

P310   *Content*
I long to canoe in December
Typescript   also 6

Contrast
see *Song*

Convalescence
see *A Rhymer's Marriage*

A Cycle of Ballades   [contents:]

P320   With laughter low the dells resound

P380 *Death*
  from *Decorations*
  Cupped in the rosey hollow of her hands
  Typescript

  Decorations
  see *Death, Marna in the Walled Garden, The Poet to the Dead*
  Queen, The Sea's Daughter

P390 *Dedicated to Delta Chi of 1900*
  We have played and toiled together
  Typescript   also 6

P400 *The Deep Blue Ocean*   September 1900
  I love the deep blue ocean
  Typescript   also 6

P410 *The Derelicts*   October 1901
  Oh! the wind is up from landward
  Typescript, pencil corrections in another hand also 6

  Doubt
  see *A Rhymer's Summer*

In a letter dated August 2, 1904:
P415 *Dream of the Poor Goat that wrote this rot*
  Manuscript, pencil, 2p., no date.

P420 *The Dreamers*
  We dreamers of wide visions know
  Dummy   7
  Typescript
P421 *Nassau Lit* 60:7 pp307ff

P430 *The Dreamer's Plea*
  Lying by the sunlit river
  Typescript   also 6

P440 *Duet (Sorry or Glad)*   November 1908
  Love thou art sorry or glad
P441   Manuscript, ink and typescript 1, also 7

  Easy Come, Easy Go
  see *Songs*

The Empty Tomb
see *Verses*

P450 *L'Envoi* June 1903
To you, fair dream, I deck my shrine
P451 Manuscript, pencil with pencil corrections,
typescript

P460 *Epitaph for M.C. not Mary Canby*
Oh she was young and she was fair
Manuscript, pencil with pencil corrections

P470 *The Face of Desire* August 1907
"Oh wherefore" saith the voice of Love
Dummy 7

The Fairy Folk
see *Untitled (Songs)*

P480 *A Fancy* 1901
Let us hold fast to the faith of our fathers
Typescript also 6

P490 *A Farewell (In an Autumn Garden)* August 1908
The garden walks are red with bloom
Manuscript, ink and typescript also 7

P500 *Finality* August 1908
Lean over, let they hair be shed
Dummy 7

Finite Love
see *Untitled*

P510 *First Frost*
The Queen unloosed the ribbands of her
silken mask
Dummy 7

P520 *First Sight*
I knew little pain of love, I knew
Dummy 7

P530 *Folly*
Folly wears a broidered robe

	Typescript	also 3, 7
P531	*Nassau Lit* 61:5 p175	
P540	*Folly's Pageant of the Dead*	
	A pageant of old poets with dumb lips	
	Typescript	also 3, 5, 7
P541	*Nassau Lit* 60:8 p370	
P550	*Foot Ball Song*	November 1901
	Good-by, Lawrenceville, you're beaten	
	Typescript	also 6
P560	*A Fragment*	
	Like the souls of those in torment	
	Typescript with ink corrections	also 6
P570	*Friendship*	
	Ye scarce may run the race of life	
	Typescript with pencil corrections	also 6
P580	*The Garden by the Sea*	July 1903
	If you should ask me where the roses grow	
	Dummy	7
	Gay-and-Twenty	
	see *Song*	
	Give O'er!	
	see *Song*	
P590	*The Golden Beaker*	
	Lord God, if one that thirsted much	
	Dummy	7
P600	*The Golf Ball*	April 1900
	There's a mother in sunny Kenwood	
	Typescript	also 6
P610	*The Great Sin*	
	Within the whirling circle of the spheres	
	Dummy	7
	Grown Wise and Old	
	see *Song*	

P710   *In Memoriam*
Far from the tempest of eternal strife
Typescript   also 6

P720   *In Memoriam*   November 1901
We knew him not, nor met him face to face
Typescript   also 6

P730   *In September*   December 1907
Shimmer of wandering wings
Dummy   7

P740   *In the Dark*   December 1907
Old thoughts rise in the dark, as
windowless towers
Dummy   7

P750   *In the Hidden Orchard*   August 1908
She holds in either hollow of her hands
Typescript   also 7

P760   *In the Saloon*
Into the temple's warm and dizzy light
Dummy   7

P770   *Insincerity*
Who weaveth him with cunning wit
Dummy   7

P780   *Into the Silent Land*   March 1905
Once came into the silent land when it
was almost night
Dummy   7

P790   *Introduction Written for CC Jr*   December 1899
Oh Goddess Muse, come listen to my song
Typescript   also 6

P800   *It Has Been Written*   March 1901
It has been written none can conquer fate
Typescript with pencil corrections   also 6

P810   *The Jester's Song*   May 1903
I built me a house of cards

	Typescript with pencil corrections	also 6
P811	*Nassau Lit* 60:2 p45–6	
P820	*June* This is a time of laughter, June hath spread Dummy	7
P830	*The King's Daughter* The feast hath lost its salt and savor Manuscript with ink corrections, typescript	December 1905 also 7
P831	*Nassau Lit* 61:8 p353	
P321	*A Lady's Face* from *A Cycle of Ballades* The battered crests and the strain and stress Typescript	2, also 7
P840	*The Lament of a Small Boy (Vacation)* Of all the sorely pestered folks Typescript with pencil corrections	1906
P850	*The Lament of a Would-Be Pessimist* I yearn to write like Edgar Poe Typescript	also 6
P860	*Lancelot to Galahault* I were athirst for battle at her whim Dummy	7
P870	*The Land Beyond the Moon* There is a land that we fain would reach Typescript	also 6
P880	*Last Love* The surging moon-grey shadows broke the white Dummy	7
P890	*Last Night* Last night the laughter in the stalls rippled out Dummy	7
P900	*Laughter* Laugh while ye may and in your mirth forget Typescript	also 6

P910   *Laughter and Tears*   August 1907
        I think there is a benison in weeping
        Dummy   7

P920   *The Leading Man*
        With kindled eyes and fragile, tremulous hands
        Dummy   7

P930   *The Liar*
        She has the subtle art of telling lies
        Dummy   7

P940   *Life*
        Right well I know the ebb and flow
        Dummy   7

P950   *Life and the Other*
        She said, "Stoop whilst I bind thy brow
        with roses"
        Nassau Lit 61:8 p328

P960   *Light Love*
        There's many a lad and lass shall love
        Dummy   7

P970   *Light Love Remembered*   August 1907
        My dreams are not of thee; I woke but now
        Typescript with pencil corrections   also 7

P980   *The Lights of Home*
        When the sea, lashed white in fury
        Typescript   also 6

P990   *Lines*
        As the wind and the sunset rain
        Nassau Lit 61:8 p351

P1000 *Lines Dedicated to a Week-End Guest*
        Abashed by fluctuating stocks
        Typescript   also 7

P1010 *Lines With a Book of Verse*
        My skill is not the skill that weaves
        Nassau Lit 61:6 p266

P1020	*The Little God*	October 1905
	I wrought a little god of clay	
	Dummy	7
P1030	*A Little Song*	July 1903
	If you should ask me where the roses grow	
	Typescript	also 6
P1040	*The Lobster Man*	October 1900
	I saw him first on Sunday night	
	Typescript	also 6
P1050	*Love Lies Hid*	September 1908
	I am a golden trumpet for the lips	
	Dummy	7
P1060	*Love Lost*	April 1904
	If love were as the passing scent	
	Dummy	7
P1070	*Love of You*	May 1909
	Though Autumn beat his muffled drum	
	Dummy	7
P1080	*Love the Gambler*	
	Love plays to win, and not alone	
	Dummy	7
	Love Vagabond	
	see *Song*	
	Love's Imminence	
	see *Songs*	
P1090	*Love's Indian Summer*	
	I came upon her unawares today	
	Dummy	7
P1100	*Love's Seasons*	
	Inconstant passion's like the winds that blow	
	Dummy	7
P1110	*Lyric*	November 1909
	I have said out my say	
	Manuscript, ink	

SVMMA IVVENTVTIS

TO CHRISTIAN GAUSS

OCTOBER dons her russet vestiture
　　Tinctured with blood of roses lately dead—
Sad robes whose deathly splendours shall endure
　　So brief a while; yet, after all is said,
Winter is likewise brief—her shroud of snows
The immaculate birth-robe of some seedling rose;

And we shall round, as always, to the spring,
　　Glad of her warmth. But still the days retain
Enough of summer's glow that one may fling
　　Repentance down, and give the loosened rein
To fancies bred of pleasant idleness
In such a place, and hazard many a guess

On Faith. And here I quite forget the din
　　Of Life—the man that some would have me be;
And since you hold my drifting hours no sin
　　I make to you my songs' apology,
Knowing, tho' somewhat tangled in its sense,
'Twill gain at least a kindly audience.

For I remember many a morning hour
　　In Alexander Street, and many a night
Beside your lamp-glow, when you poured the dower
　　Of wider reading forth for my delight;
How, often, tho' I shirked the tasks you set
I found your kindness ready to forget

Kenneth Sawyer Goodman

THE CALL OF AUTUMN

Somewhere beyond the hills
   Someone is calling;
Soft by the autumn rills
   Bright leaves are falling;

Woodlands are all ablaze
   Crimson and yellow;
Birds call across the maize
   Each to his fellow;

Restless feet tap the floor
   Eager for speeding;
Eyes seek the open door,
   Listless, unheeding.

Love, I may bide no more,
   Lost days requiting;
Wonderland spreads its store
   Dim and inviting.

Summertide's glow is lost;
   Wide, windy spaces
Thrill with the coming frost;
   Lure of strange places

Rings in the swaying pine
   Noontide and gloaming,
Setting this heart of mine
   Once more a-roaming.

SAMPLE PAGES FROM *A RIVEN LUTE* (COLL. 7)

P1115 *Mag in the Well*
Manuscript, pencil, 1p., no date.

P1120 *The Makers of Rime*   December 1904
God said to the Makers of Rime
Dummy   7

P1130 *The Man Behind the Gun*   September 1900
With the "Man Behind the Gun"
Typescript   also 6

P1140 *Marna in the Walled Garden*
from *Decorations*
He said, "Thy life and mine shall be
Typescript   also 7

P1150 *Mary's Lamb*   April 1901
Mary has a little lamb
Typescript   also 6

P1160 *A Modern Dinner*   February 1911
A table past the columns — here we dine
Dummy   7

P1170 *A Moment*
Behind the flame of the match as you
lighted your cigarette
Dummy   7

P1180 *My Fifty Dollar Jag*
"If we were rich," some fellows say
Typescript   also 6

P1190 *The New Year*
Beyond the wreaths of silver stars
Typescript   also 3, 4, 7
P1191 *Nassau Lit* 60:6 p231

P1200 *The New Year*
"Rejoice," they cry, "A new year has been born."
Typescript   also 6

P1210 *No Master*   January 1901
When we've played it out to the finish
Typescript   also 6

P1220 *A Norse Love Song*   December 1904
       Love! I am freer than the strong white wings
       Typescript   also 6, 7
P1221   Manuscript, pencil, in unknown hand
P1225   *Nassau Lit* 59:5 p253
P1226   *Princeton Verse,* edited by Raymond B. Fosdick.
          Buffalo, N.Y.: Hausauer, Son & Jones, 1904, p. 136 [X]

       November
          see *A Rhymer's Marriage*

       Nuits de Juin
          see *After Victor Hugo*

P1230 *October*
       also called *Song*
       Bright lips I might have kissed
P1231   Manuscript, ink and typescript

P1240 *October*   December 1907
       "Once more, for the last time, my dear!
       Dummy   7

P1250 *Old Friends*
       Old Friends, I prize far more than love
       Dummy   6

P1260 *The Old Gods*   September 1905
       Out of the wild fantastic disarray
       Dummy   7

P1270 *The Old Story*
       'Tis but the old, old story of the garden
       Typescript   also 3, 4
P1271   *Nassau Lit* 60:3 p87

P1280 *On Taking Cold Baths in the Morning*
       I rise reluctantly at seven:forty
       Dummy   7

P1290 *Out of the Dust*   November 1909
       Out of the dust in the cathedral crypt
       Dummy   7

P1300   *Out of the Mist*
Out of the mist that shrouds, O friend,
Dummy   7

P1310   *Parsimony*   December 1910
I am weary and sore oppressed
Dummy   7

P1320   *The Parting of the Ways*
The guests have gone from the banquet
Typescript with pencil corrections   also 6

P1330   *The People o' Dreams*
I have seen them beckon and glimmer
P1331   Manuscript, ink and typescript   also 3, 4, 7
P1332   *Nassau Lit* 61:2 p68

P1340   *Phaon*   December 1906
Love, I shall bind dark myrtle in thine hair
Dummy   7

P1350   *Pierrette*   January 1906
I asked one little boon of Love, and Love
Dummy   7
P1351   *Nassau Lit* 61:7 p311

P1360   *The Piper*   May 1908
I heard him when the east was white
P1361   Manuscript ink with pencil corrections, typescript   1, also 7

P1370   *The Play is Done*
Strike not the chords of longing and regret
Typescript   also 6

P1380   *The Poet to the Dead Queen*
from *Decorations*
Oh, Queen, the haggard winds carouse
Typescript   also 6

P1390   *Pondering*   January 1902
Faith is departed, and here in the gloaming
Typescript   also 6

P1400   *Postscript*
from *A Rhymer's Summer*

A year they lay upon the shelves
Typescript   also 7

P1410 *The Pride of Honor*   March 1901
The days of our blindness are over
Typescript with pencil corrections   also 6

P1420 *The Pride of Honor*
Strong is the pride of our honor
Typescript

P1430 *Prophecy*
Some day I shall make songs that will ring true
Dummy   7

P1440 *A Question*   June 1901
Why ponder ye what none may understand
Typescript   also 6

P1450 *Qui Multam Amavit*
I think the autumn silence, and revealment
Typescript   also 7

Quia Pulves Es
see *After Victor Hugo*

Reading thy Rimes
see *Rondel (to A B)*

P1460 *Regret*   October 1908
You waited patiently. I think
Dummy   7

P1470 *Retreat*
The apple trees will be in bloom
Dummy   7

P1480 *A Reverie*   April 1901
The weary brain with myriad fancies teams [sic]
Typescript with pencil corrections   also 6

P1490 *A Rhymer Marries*
Morn; and the shimmer of amber sands
Dummy   7

A Rhymer's Marriage [contents:]

P1500	Night; and the fingers of light winds astir	
P1501	The times I've gone afield for flowers *(Convalescence)*	
P1502	Underneath the flinching stars *(November)*	
P1503	The wrens were at your windowsill	
	Typescripts	also 7

A Rhymer's Summer [contents:]

P1510	The sea is mad with a shimmer of winds and wings *(Autumn Noon)*	
P1511	We read today in an orchard beside the brook *(Doubt)*	
P1400	A year they lay upon the shelves *(Postscript)*	
	Typescripts	also 7

P1520	*A Rimer's* [sic] *Summer*	March 1909
	Here is a wreath of little songs I made	
	Dummy	7

P1530	*Rivalry*	
	He, being dead, hath wrought on her	
	Dummy	7

P1540	*The Robe of Dreams*	
	I wrought a Robe of fairy woof	
	Nassau Lit 61:7 p277	

P335	*Rondel*	September 1907
	from *A Cycle of Ballades*	
	Oh Death! Men fear thee much	
P335a	Manuscript, ink	2, also 5

P331	*Rondel*	September 1907
	from *A Cycle of Ballades*	
	Only awhile: Though Life be sweet	
	Typescript	2

P330	*Rondel (to A B) (Reading thy Rimes)*	September 1907
	from *A Cycle of Ballades*	
	Reading thy rhymes, oh brother, I have grown	
	Typescript	2, also 7

P332	*Rondel*	September 1907
	from *A Cycle of Ballades*	
	Touching her lips, I dreamed a bitter dream	
	Typescript	2
P336	*Rondel*	September 1907
	from *A Cycle of Ballades*	
	What of the dead, have they nor mirth nor tears	
P336a	Manuscript, ink and typescript	2
P1550	*A Rose and the Star*	
	A rose, so they say, for a day	
	Typescript	also 3
P1551	*Nassau Lit* 61:1 p36	
P1560	*The Rose and the Star*	August 1903
	This is the song a red rose sang a star	
	Manuscript with pencil corrections, typescript	
P1561	with pencil corrections	also 6, 7
	Roseate Life	
	see *Villanelle*	
P1570	*Roses (Roses Red and White)*	
	From kisses that left a burning mark of	
	their passing	
	Typescript	also 7
P1571	*Nassau Lit* 61:2 p77	
	Roses Red and White	
	see *Roses*	
P1575	*Sans Souci*	
	I sing no song of long ago	7
P1580	*The Sea's Daughter*	
	from *Decorations*	
	The blind blue wave goes over lips and eyes	
	Typescript	also 7
P1590	*Secrecies*	
	On the jet mirrors of the night are cast	
	Dummy	7

Separation
　　see *Songs*

P1600　*Shelley*
　　　　A leaping flame, a thunder of quick wings
　　　　Dummy　　　　　　　　　　　　　　　　　　　　7

P1610　*Silence*　　　　　　　　　　　　　　　　　September 1906
　　　　She hath not moved for these five hours
　　　　Dummy　　　　　　　　　　　　　　　　　　　　7

P1620　*Sing a Song*
　　　　Cock an eye and take a chance
　　　　Manuscript, pencil on the letterhead of
　　　　　　William O. Goodman

P1630　*The Singer*
　　　　Down through the autumn forest
　　　　Typescript　　　　　　　　　　　　　　　　also 3, 7
P1631　*Nassau Lit* 60:4 p167

　　　　A Singer's Masque　　　　　　　　　　　September 1907
　　　　see *A Masque* in the bibliography of plays of
　　　　K S Goodman

P1230　*Song (Bright Lips, Light Heart) (October)*　　December 1908
　　　　Bright lips I might have kissed in May
　　　　Typescript　　　　　　　　　　　　　　　　also 7

P1640　*Song (Contrast)*
　　　　I came into the garden-close
　　　　Typescript　　　　　　　　　　　　　　　　also 3, 4, 7
P1641　*Nassau Lit* 61:3 p89

P1650　*Song (Gay-and-Twenty)*　　　　　　　　August 1905
　　　　Laughter, only laughter?
P1651　Manuscript, ink and typescript　　　　also 3, 7

P1660　*Song (Give O'er!)*　　　　　　　　　　　March 1906
　　　　Give o'er thy quest. It shall not bide for long
　　　　Typescript　　　　　　　　　　　　　　　　also 7

P1670　*Song (Grown Wise and Old)*　　　　　　May 1908
　　　　They do not love as we, nor sing togeather [sic]

P1671	Typescript, manuscript, ink	also 7
P1680	*Song*	
	I knew she was not there, yet crept	
P1681	Manuscript, ink and typescript	also 3
P1682	*Nassau Lit* 61:9 p391	
P1690	*Song (Love Vagabond)*	September 1909
	Low above the paling foam	
	Manuscript, ink	1, also 7
P1700	*Song*	
	Only the moon and seven stars	
P1701	Manuscript, ink and typescript	
P1710	*Song (Weariness)*	November 1906
	It is not love that I desire	
P1711	Manuscript, ink and typescript	also 5, 7
P1720	*Song (April and December)*	
	I walked her way and chaffed her	
	Typescript	also 7
P1730	*Song*	
	She walks no more among the slender roses	
	Nassau Lit 61:6 p264	
P1740	*Song from the Queen's Tragedy*	
	Ages ago, Oh Sweet, we met	
P1741	Manuscript, ink and typescript	also 3
P1750	*A Song of Content*	
	Lounging here in the sun	
	Dummy	7
P1760	*The Song of Faith*	May 1903
	Out of the darkness that follows the gloaming	
	Typescript with pencil corrections	also 6
P1770	*The Song of the Rankers*	January 1902
	Some of us chaps were too lazy	
	Typescript	also 6
P1780	*The Song of the Sword*	March 1901
	The days are gone wherein my glory lay	
	Typescript	also 6

P1790 *Song Written for the Harvard School Golf*   June 1901
         Team of 1901
         Oh now we'll cheer for Harvard School
         Typescript   also 6

P1800 *Songs (Apart)*
         Oh Lassie, every thought of you
         Typescript   also 7

P1810 *Songs (Because of You)*
         I sang, when birds were mating
         Typescript   also 7

P1820 *Songs (Easy Come, Easy Go)*
         There's many a lad and lass that know
         Typescript   also 7

P1830 *Songs (Love's Imminence)*
         The moon-rays dapple all the forest reaches
         Typescript   also 7
P1831 *Nassau Lit* 61:1 pp15–16

P1840 *Songs*
         Oh, to be up and roving
         Typescript   also 5

P1850 *Songs (Separation)*
         The Moon, that rides the raveled night
         Typescript   also 7

P1860 *Songs (When the Rose Withereth)*   May 1907
         When the rose withereth, what then, My Lady?
         Typescript   also 5, 7

P1870 *A Sonnet on the Goose Family*   January 1902
         I'm sick of all the tribe of goose
         Typescript   also 6

         Sorry or Glad
         see *Duet*

P1880 *The Spinner*   December 1906
         She sits at twilight spinning
P1881   Manuscript, ink and typescript   also 5, 7

P1890 *Spring Magic*
　　　　Shall life outlast desire of her?
　　　　Dummy　　　　　　　　　　　　　　　7

P1900 *Summa Juventutis*
　　　　October dons her russet vestiture
　　　　Typescript　　　　　　　　　　　　also 7

P1910 *Summer in Arcady*　　　　　　　November 1906
　　　　No thought for cloudy days hereafter
P1911 Manuscript, ink and typescript　　also 5

P1920 *Summer Songs (Summer Trysts)*　September 1904
　　　　Wan star-light over waters pale with sleep
P1921 Manuscript, ink and typescript　　also 3, 7

　　　　Summer Trysts
　　　　see *Summer Songs*

P1930 *Temptation*　　　　　　　　　　May 1901
　　　　Alone we stand upon the brink of Time
　　　　Typescript　　　　　　　　　　　　also 6

P1940 *Tennyson's Dreams*
　　　　Dreams, only dreams woven on looms of gold
　　　　Typescript　　　　　　　　　　　　also 6

　　　　Terminus
　　　　see *Untitled*

P1950 *The Three Apples*　　　　　　　December 1905
　　　　Three golden apples hang to the bough
P1951 Manuscript, ink and typescript　　also 3, 4, 7

P1960 *The Tides*　　　　　　　　　　January 1908
　　　　Lips alive with a name
　　　　Dummy　　　　　　　　　　　　　　　7

P1965 *Tiny and Dan*
　　　　Manuscript, pencil, 2p., no date.

P1970 *To a Dancing Girl*
　　　　You said: "If I might dance my fill
　　　　Dummy　　　　　　　　　　　　　　　7

81

P1980 *To a Lady*   November 1909
To kiss your hand at new Love's birth
Dummy   7

P1990 *To an Old Love*   September 1907
There is a stream of Dreams my dear
P1991 Manuscript, ink and typescript   also 5, 7

P2000 *A Toast*   February 1901
Oh Bacchus, lend new sparkle to the wine
Typescript   also 6

P2010 *Today and Tomorrow*   June 1906
I wonder, when God wrought the land
P2011 Manuscript, ink, typescript with pencil
corrections
P2012 *Nassau Lit* 61:9 pp371–6   also 7

P2020 *The Toiler*
I have woven many garlands out of many happy
Dummy   7

P2030 *Too Late*
Peace awoke her soul
Dummy   7

P333 *Triad*   September 1907
from *A Cycle of Ballades*
My dear, the subtle key
Typescript   2

P2040 *Tristram in Brittany*
Passion is changeful as the changeful moon
Typescript, pencil corrections in another hand   also 7

P2050 *Twilight Song*
The touch of the twilight lingers
Dummy   7

Ultimate
see *Ballade*

P2060 *Unanswered*   August 1908
What is this Fame men strive for, Brother mine
Dummy   7

P2070 *Unavailing*   July 1908
         I wove an airy mesh of rhyme
         Dummy   7

P2080 *Untitled*
         A. a is for all of us out for a lark
         Manuscript, ink

P2085 *Untitled*
         Dearest Paul, I thank you.
         Manuscript, ink, 2 p.

P2090 *Untitled*
         Gwen & Bill go up the hill
         Manuscript, ink

P2100 *Untitled*
         A's for arrival, I'm here with a smash
         Typescript

P1830 *Untitled* (Part II of *Songs: (Love's Imminence),* q.v.)
         The fairy folk are out again tonight
         Typescript
P1831 *Nassau Lit* 61:1 pp 15-16

P2120 *Untitled (Terminus)*   May 1908
         Love passes lightly dancing with the throng
         Manuscript, ink   also 1, 7

P2130 *Untitled*
         The moon had faltered from the sky bending
         Typescript

P2140 *Untitled*
         Oh, follow me! Oh, follow me!
         Typescript

P2150 *Untitled (Finite Love)*   May 1909
         This much at least I know of her
         Manuscript, pencil   1, also 7

P2160 *Untitled*
         We're going back to Princeton
         Typescript

P2170 *Untitled*
When all sweet things and all things sad
Typescript   also 3
P2171 *Nassau Lit* 61:5 p215

P320 *Untitled*
from *A Cycle of Ballades*
With laughter low the dells resound
Typescript, initialed DCV [Donald Cuyler Vaughn]

P322 *Untitled*
from *A Cycle of Ballades*
At Woodstock, flanked by moor and fen
Typescript

Untitled
Night; and the fingers of light winds astir
see *A Rhymer's Marriage*

Vacation
see *The Lament of a Small Boy*

P2180 *Vale Amor*   May 1907
Oh once – beloved, if ever for thy sake
Typescript, pencil corrections in another hand   also 7

P2190 *Verses (In After Time)*   March 1906
In after time if some new love should quicken
P2191 Manuscript, ink (March), typescript   also 3, 7
(dated September)

P2200 *Verses (The Empty Tomb)*   December 1904
Our laughter echo in an empty tomb
P2201 Manuscript, ink and typescript   also 3, 7

P328 *Villanelle (Roseate Life)*
from *A Cycle of Ballades*
Red lips and ruddy wine   2, also 5

P334 *Villanelle*   September 1907
from *A Cycle of Ballades*
A little laughter and a little love   2, also 5

P324	*Villanelle (Winter's Guerdons)*	October 1906
	from *A Cycle of Ballades*	
	A little laughter for the yesteryear	
	Typescript	2, also 7
P2220	*The Voices of the Fates*	
	Alas I hear the voices of them calling;	
	Nassau Lit 61:6 p227	
P2230	*Wakefulness*	
	Oh ye with waking eyes, who keep	
	Dummy	7
P2240	*What?*	May 1903
	What is it prompts our hand to smite	
	Manuscript, pencil, typescript with pencil	
	corrections	also 6
P2250	*When Charley Plays the Game*	
	If you should see a cloud of dust	
	Typescript	6
	When the Rose Withereth	
	see *Songs*	
P2260	*While We Are Young*	
	Grey Saints be silent of the dim	
	Typescript	also 3, 7
P2261	*Nassau Lit* 61:5 p213	
P2270	*The Wide Road*	
	Not mine to make love's pallid lips respire	
P2271	Manuscript, ink and typescript	also 5, 7
	Winter's Guerdons	
	see *Villanelle*	
P327	*With a Book of Verse*	October 1906
	from *A Cycle of Ballades*	
	Heed this my singing, which is part of me	
P327a	Manuscript, ink and typescript	2, also 5, 7
P2280	*A Woman's Friendship*	
	If I might make you any song	
	Dummy	7

The Wrens
　　see *A Rhymer's Marriage*

P2290 *Youth*
　　Oh, ivory breast where little veins of blue
　　Dummy　　　　　　　　　　　　　　　　　　7

P2300 *Zabricka*　　　　　　　　　　　　　　February 1901
　　He saw her first on the street-car
　　Typescript　　　　　　　　　　　　　　　also 6

DRAWING OF THREE STANDING MEN (M230)

DIARIES

D10 [Diary Number One]

My Trip Abroad
"This Book
    belongs to
        K. Sawyer Goodman
            5026 Greenwood Ave
                Chicago Ill
                U.S.A.
and is a brief & serious
narrative of the F.G.M. personaly [sic]
conducted Funny-house on
its travels, and its doings
wise and otherwise.
                        authors note."
January 2 - March 24, 1907.
[135] pp., unpaged after p. 95
On lined paper with gilt edge, in red binding
marked with gold leaf.

D20 [Diary Number Two]

"I only began to keep this up as a Regular Line
a day book on February 4th 1909. The Entries
for December 1908. & January 1909 are made

"1/28 Cairo (Gizeh).

We visited points of interest. Went down to sphinx and granite temple escorted by numerous bedouins, importunate but courteous and good-natured. Elinor and I took several Kodak pictures and rode camels. Camels are not so uncomfortable to ride as I had supposed. Boon and I went into the great Pyramid. Spooky trip but great fun, very slippery and footing bad. Have to stoop all the first two thirds of the way. Each of us had three arabs: one to push, one to pull, and one to yell."

EGYPT, 1907: EXCERPTS FROM DIARY (D10) AND
PHOTOGRAPH ALBUM. PHOTOGRAPH (LEFT TO RIGHT):
UNIDENTIFIED, KENNETH SAWYER GOODMAN, UNIDENTIFIED,
ERNA SAWYER GOODMAN, WILLIAM OWEN GOODMAN ("BOON"),
ELINOR MEECHAM

up from memory & from my engagement book,
being therefore incomplete. ~~The entries for
December 1908 will be found at the back of
the book.~~"

January 1, 1909 - December 31, 1911.
[191] pp., unpaged
In Graves' "Double-Indexed Diary,"
crosshatched paper, in black leather binding.

D30   [Diary Number Three]

"Kenneth Sawyer Goodman
   ~~5026 Greenwood Ave Chicago Ill~~
      or
917 ~~1027~~ Railway Exchange Bld
       Chicago Ill.
      or
10 East Schiller Street Chicago
continuation of record kept in
another book since Jan 1st 1909.

    This Book was begun
January 1st 1912

<u>suitable reward will be given</u>
<u>for the return of this book</u>
to the above address."

January 1, 1912 - December 31, 1916.
[367] pp., unpaged
In "A Line a Day,"
ruled paper with gilt edge, bound in leather
and marked with gold leaf.

DRAWING OF TWO MEN LEANING AND SMOKING (M270)

SHORT STORIES AND ARTICLES

At the Castle of Dawn

S10   *Nassau Lit* 60:8 pp348–352

Cartwright's Burglary

S20   Manuscript. *"Cartwright's Burglary"* [first page] . [Cover:]
          "Cartwright's Burglary. 'Nassau Lit' K. Sawyer Goodman"
          14p., ink, no date.
S21   *Nassau Lit* 61:2 pp62–67

A Fable

S25   *Nassau Lit* 61:1 pp 37–38

The Garden

S30   Manuscript. *The Garden* [first page] . [Cover:] *"The Garden. K. Sawyer
          Goodman 06. 86 Nassau Street."*
          10p., ink. With corrections and comments in another hand.
S31   *Nassau Lit* 60:3 pp98–102
S32   Typescript. *The Garden.* [5] p., no date. With appended poem initialed
          D[onald] C[uyler] V[aughn] .
S33   Typescript. *The Garden.* [5] p., no date. [3 carbon copies of above, less
          the appended poem]

On the Wings of the Enemy

S35 Typescript. *On the Wings of the Enemy.* 12p., no date.
S36 Manuscript. *Story. On the Wings of the Enemy.*
20p., ink, no date.

The Queen's Tragedy

with Donald Cuyler Vaughn
S37 *Nassau Lit* 61:3 pp102-111 (Foreword)
Nassau Lit 61:4 pp149-156 (Part II)
Nassau Lit 61:5 pp176-183 (Conclusion)

The Sargasso Company

S40 Typescript. *The Sargasso Company.* 4p., no date. With attached note on the letterhead of Thomas Wood Stevens, and in his hand, summarizing the story. [Pencil, 2p., no date]

The Three Who Knew

with Donald Cuyler Vaughn
S50 *Nassau Lit* 60:4 pp133-139 (part I)
Nassau Lit 60:5 pp192-196 (part II)

Untitled Short Story No. 1

S60 Manuscript. 2p., ink, no date.

Untitled Short Story No. 2

S70 Manuscript. pp. 5-10, pencil, no date.

Untitled Article

S80 Manuscript. 8 [12] p., pencil, no date.
Regarding the production and staging of pageants.

Cousin Jim

A film by John T. McCutcheon and Kenneth Sawyer Goodman.
S90 Manuscript. *Cousin Jim. A Comedy Melodrama.* 39p., ink with pencil corrections, no date. [in 119 scenes]

S91 Typescript. *Cousin Jim. A Comedy Melodrama.* 23p., with pencil corrections, no date. [in 119 scenes]

Drama: The Chicago Theatre Society

S100 Article in *The Nation* 98:2542, March 19, 1914
by Kenneth Sawyer Goodman

Student Papers

S110 *Addison. For B. Tuckerman. March 6th 1906.*
K Sawyer Goodman
86 Nassau Street
Princeton
Manuscript, ink, with corrections in another hand.
Also pencil notations and drawings by KSG. 6p.

S111 *Balzac. French Lit. May 15th 1906.*
K Sawyer Goodman
86 Nassau Street
Princeton.
Manuscript, ink. 6p.

S112 *Chesterfield. For Mr. Tuckerman. April 23rd 1906.*
K. Sawyer Goodman
—86 Nassau Street—
Princeton N.J.
Manuscript, ink, with corrections in another hand. 6p.

S113 *Edward Gibbon. March 26th 1906.*
K. Sawyer Goodman.
86 Nassau Street
Manuscript, ink. 5p.

S114 *First Reading of Spencers Faery Queene*
Manuscript, ink, with pencil corrections in another hand. 6p. [incomplete]

S115 *Outline of Burkes Speech on Conciliation with America. April 2nd 1906.*
K. Sawyer Goodman
86 Nassau Street
Princeton
Manuscript, ink. 7p.

S116 *Theme on Romeo & Juliet to make up absence from test.*
K. Sawyer Goodman.
Manuscript, ink. [3] p.

Gossip (regular column)

S120	*Nassau Lit:* 61:1 pp41–42	S125	*Nassau Lit:* 61:6 pp270–271
S121	*Nassau Lit:* 61:2 pp81–82	S126	*Nassau Lit:* 61:7 pp316–317
S122	*Nassau Lit:* 61:3 pp126–127	S127	*Nassau Lit:* 61:8 pp357–358
S123	*Nassau Lit:* 61:4 pp168–169	S128	*Nassau Lit:* 61:9 pp395–396
S124	*Nassau Lit:* 61:5 pp220–221		

The Legend of St. Juliana

S130 Review in *Nassau Lit* 61:8 pp363–364

DRAWING OF SEATED MAN WITH CANE
AND STARING MAN (M160)

MISCELLANEOUS WORKS

M10   Booklet. *Portraits without Pictures. by A Cubist* [KSG?]
Westbrook: Wee Bum Team Match, June 28th, 1913. [16] p.

M20   Broadside. *NOTeUS!* Dated "Sept. 2nd."

M25   Contract. Between Washington Square Players, Kenneth Sawyer Goodman and Ben Hecht. Signed by Hecht, Goodman, and Edward Goodman
(secretary of the Washington Square Players). With notes in the hand of
EG, initialed by him and KSG. December 30, 1916.

[All sizes are given in inches]

M30   Drawing. Buildings near Canal. 5½x7, pencil on paper.

M35   Drawing. Cat and Bear. 3½x5½, pencil. Framed. [X]

M40   Drawing. Couple With Potted Plant. 5½x7, ink. Marked "cut 3 page 4."
Caption: *Splash. James dear where shall we put our Wedding notices?
Oh, put them in the scrapbook.*

M41   *Tiger* 16:5 p16.

M50   Drawing. Dressed Man in Bed. 14¾x20, oil pastel on paper.

M60   Drawing. Egyptian characters. 8¼x22¼, ink design on lamp shade.

M65   Drawing. *The Fortnightly Club.* 5x8½, ink. Signed "K.S. Goodman."

M70   Drawing. Four Woodland Sketches. Pencil and charcoal on paper, pinned
together. Three each 5½x8½, one 9x12.

M80   Drawing. For Ephraim and the Winged Bear. 5½x7½, ink. Framed. [X]

M90   Drawing. Girl Leaving Home. 14¾x20, oil pastel on paper.

M100 Drawing. Initial *B*. 5x5¾, ink. (drawing dimensions, 2x2). Marked "Cut 2 page 2. Initial letter to editorial."

M110 Drawing. Island Under Moonlight. 14¾x20, oil pastel on paper.

M120 Drawing. Knight with Flag. 11½x15, ink. Marked with KSG monogram.

M130 Drawing. Man Smoking. 1¾x6½, ink. Signed with KSG monogram.

M140 Drawing. Man with Cane, Plus Women and Potted Trees. In two pieces, 5½x7¾ and 4½x5½, ink. Marked "Cut 12 page 12. Heading for story the 'Blue Hose'."

M141 *Tiger* 16:2 p12.

M150 Drawing. Mrs. Goodman [?] crying. 9x12, pencil on paper. Dated "Dec. '16."

M155 Drawing. Seated Knight. 3½x4½, ink. Marked "cut 22 page 15." Signed "K.S.G."

M160 Drawing. Seated Man with Cane and Staring Man. 4x6¼, ink. Signed "K.S. Goodman '06."

M170 Drawing. Sophomore Class. 9¼x14½, ink and pencil. Signed "K.S. Goodman '06."

M180 Drawing. Still Life with Bird (obverse), Two Vessels (reverse). Marked "Miss Coe & Miss McCally." Signed "K.S. Goodman" on reverse. 12x19, charcoal on paper.

M190 Drawing. Still Life With Fruit. 13x18½, charcoal on paper.

M200 Drawing. Stone Railroad Bridge. 15x20, oil pastel on paper.

M210 Drawing. Suffragette. 9x12, oil pastel on paper.

M220 Drawing. Three Jews. 5x8½, ink. Caption: *Chorus of Israelites: Vot a business college is dot Princeton!!"* Marked "Cut 5 Page 5." Signed "K.S.G."

M221 *Tiger* 16:2 p5.

M230 Drawing. Three Standing Men. 5x6, ink. Signed "K.S.G." With attached caption in another hand.

M231 *Tiger* 16:5 p24.

M240 Drawing. Two Baseball Players. 7½x8, ink. Caption: *Muggsy — Wat yez sore about yez didn't lose. Mickey — Mag thru me down cause I let another goil chew me gum after de game, see!* Marked "cut 9 page 8."

M241 *Tiger* 16:2 p8.

M250 Drawing. Two bears. 3¾x5½, pencil. Signed with KSG monogram. Framed. [X]

M260 Drawing. Two men and dog. 6x6, ink. Caption (in another hand): *Gas L. Does your grandfather use a cane? No, indeed, his shoe is his sole support.* Marked "cut 10 page 7." Signed "K.S.G."

M261 *Tiger* 16:5 p19.

M270 Drawing. Two Men, Leaning and Smoking. 6¼x7½, ink. Caption: *1st S.S. Fine excuse Jim took up to the committee last week. 2nd S.S. Where did he get it. 1st S.S. From the Dean.* Marked "cut VI page 5." With KSG monogram.

M271 *Tiger* 16:5 p17.

M280 Drawing. Two Men, One Smoking. 5x5, ink. Signed "K.S.G." Marked "cut 5 page 4."

M281 *Tiger* 16:5 p16.

M290 Drawing. Two Men with Coats. 6x6½, ink. Caption: *Jim — Say how did you wear the nap off your coat. Spike — Sleeping in it.* Marked "cut 12 page 7."

M291 *Tiger* 16:5 p19.

M300 Drawing. Two Men with Potted Tree. 5x6, ink. Signed "K.S.G." Marked "Cut 7 page 5."

M310 Drawing. Uncle Sam. 4½x7, ink with water color. Caption (in another hand): *Uncle Sam: see what I do to objectionalb* [sic] *people.*

M320 Drawing. William O. Goodman in two poses: Front View (reverse) and Side View (obverse). 19x24½, oil pastel on paper.

M330 Drawing. William O. Goodman, side view. 19x25, oil pastel on paper.

M340 Drawing. William O. Goodman Sleeping. 6x8¼, pencil on paper.

M350 Drawing. Woman and Potted Trees. 6x7½, ink. Marked "Cut 1. page 1. Same Size."

M360 Drawing. Woman Seated. 9x12, pencil on paper. Dated "Dec -16-."

M370 Drawing. Woman with Large Muff. 3¼x5, ink. Signed "K.S. Goodman '06." Framed.

M371 *Tiger* 16:5 p13.

M373 Drawing. Woman with muff and two men. 3¼x4¼, ink. Marked "cut IV page 4." Signed "KSG."

M374 Drawings. For Princeton and Hill School publications. Various sizes. Ink, pencil, oil pastel on paper or board. 18 pieces (some obverse and reverse) for *The Dial,* signed "K.S. Goodman" or "KG" monogram, dated " '02." 11 pieces (one obverse and reverse) for unspecified publication, signed "K.S. Goodman" or "K.S.G.," dated " '06." 3 pieces unspecified, one unsigned, one "KG" monogram, one "K.S. Goodman," no dates. Slip-cased *Sketches – Kenneth Sawyer Goodman.* [X]

M375 Drawings. For the *Princeton Tiger.*

Volume	Number	Size	Page
13	6	2x5	132
13	7	2x2½	172
13	8	3x4	178
13	9	2x5	207
13	9	1½x2½	211
13	9	3x3	212
14	1	1x2½	6
14	2	2½x4½	6
14	2	2½x3½	13
14	3	3x5	5
14	3	2½x3	13
14	3	1¾x3	15
14	4	2½x5	4
14	4	2¼x7	6
14	4	2½x5	8
14	4	2x4½	15
14	4	2½x5	16
14	4	2½x5¼	16
14	4	2¾x4½	20
14	4	2½x3	21 (his?)
14	5	2½x5	4

	14	5	2x2½	5
	14	5	2½x5½	10
	14	5	2¼x2¾	12
	14	6	2x5	5
	14	6	1¾x2½	6
	14	6	2x5	12
	14	6	3x5	13
	14	7	2½x2½	5
	14	7	1¾x2½	12
	14	7	3¼x5	15
	14	8	1½x2¼	8
	14	9	1¾x2½	5
	14	9	1¼x2½	6
	14	10	3½x4	half-title (1)
	14	10	2x2½	9
	14	10	1¾x2½	15
	14	10	3x5	17 (his?)
	14	10	2½x3¼	23
	14	10	2¾x4	29
	14	10	2¾x4¼	31
	15	1	2¼x2½	5
	15	4	2¼x2¼	6
	15	6	2½x2½	5
	15	6	1¼x5	11
	15	6	2x2	13
	15	7	1½x2¼	14
	15	9	1¾x2¼	6
	15	9	2x2½	11
	16	1	2x2½	4
	16	1	1¼x5	7
	16	1	2½x2¾	11
M221	16	2	2¾x4¾	5
M241	16	2	3½x4	8
M141	16	2	1½x5	12
	16	4	2¾x4½	19
	16	4	2½x2¾	28
	16	4	2x2½	28
	16	4	2½x2½	29
	16	4	2¼x2¾	30

M371	16	5	7x10	title
M41	16	5	2½x3	16
M281	16	5	2¼x2½	16
M271	16	5	2½x3¼	17
M261	16	5	2½x2½	19
M291	16	5	2½x3½	19
M231	16	5	2x2¼	24
	16	5	2x2¼	27
	16	6	7x10	title
	16	6	1¼x1½	14
	16	6	2¾x5	16
	16	6	2¼x3	16
	16	6		18
	16	6	2x2½	19
	16	6	1¾x2¼	23
	16	6	2½x4	27
	16	7	1½x2½	17
	16	7	2¼x2½	28
	16	8	7x10	cover
	16	8	4½x5¾	title (his?)
	16	8	2x2¼	16
	16	8	2½x3	17
	16	8	2¼x2½	17
	16	8	1¾x2¼	19
	16	9	2¼x4¾	17
	16	9	2¼x2½	17
	16	9	2x2½	18
	16	9	2¾x2¾	18
	16	9	2x2¾	22
	16	9	2½x2½	22
	16	9	2¼x4	23
	16	9	1¾x2½	29
	16	9	2¼x2½	30
	16	10	2½x3	32 (his?)

M376 Drawings. For the *Princeton Bric-a-Brac*, 1906.

Page	Size
Half-title	2½x5
[44]	1½x5
95	2¼x5

	119	4x5
	195	2½x3
	197	3¼x4
	[262]	3x4½
M65	270	3x5
	288	1½x5¼
	[349]	4x5
	350	1¼x2¼
	352	1¼x1½
	353	1½x2¼
	354	1¼x1½
	356	1¼x2

M380 Letter. From B. Iden Payne to Kenneth Sawyer Goodman, April 26, 1914.

M390 Letter. From Christian Gauss to Kenneth Sawyer Goodman, November 23, 1907.

M400 Letter. From Christian Gauss to Kenneth Sawyer Goodman, January 2, 1912.

M405 Letter. From Holland Hudson [Washington Square Players] to Kenneth Sawyer Goodman, January 3, 1917.

M407 Letters. From KSG to Mary Shumway.
January 17, 1904; July 20, 19[?] (not mailed); August 23, 1903; May 8, 1904; August 2, 1904; August 8, 1904; August 17, 19[04]; September 9, 1904; January 6, 1905; October 2, 1904; November 12, 1905; December 10, 1905; April 18, 1906; November 2, 19[05]; October 23, 1905; October 11, 1905; October 8, 1905; May 18, 1905; May 10, 1905; April 16, 1905; February 26, 1905; January 22, 1905; January 15, 1905. Plus a miscellaneous page marked "10," reading "Hello-o, good-bye" (no date).

M410 Letter. From Kenneth Sawyer Goodman to Miss Florence Griswold, September 17, 1915.

M420 Letter. From Kenneth Sawyer Goodman to Thomas Wood Stevens, April 10, 19[?]. [photocopy] [AZ]

M430 Letter. From Kenneth Sawyer Goodman to Thomas Wood Stevens, May 2, 19[?]. [photocopy] [AZ]

M440 Letter. From Kenneth Sawyer Goodman to Thomas Wood Stevens, June 16, 19[?]. [photocopy] [AZ]

M450 Letter. From Kenneth Sawyer Goodman to Wallace Rice, March 13, 1918.

M460 Letter. From Martyn Johnson to Kenneth Sawyer Goodman, May 3, 1913.

M465 Letter. From Maude Hume to Kenneth Sawyer Goodman, November 23, 19[?].

M468 Letter. From Thomas Wood Stevens to Kenneth Sawyer Goodman, May 16, 1911. [photocopy] [AZ]

M470 Letter. From Thomas Wood Stevens to Kenneth Sawyer Goodman, September 25, 1914. [photocopy] [AZ]

M480 Letter. From Thomas Wood Stevens to Kenneth Sawyer Goodman, June 18, 1915.

M490 Letter. From Thomas Wood Stevens to Kenneth Sawyer Goodman, July 13, 1916. [photocopy] [AZ]

[Letters. For others, see Scrapbook of Hill School, **M760**.]

M500 List of Plays. Manuscript in the hand of KSG. No date.

M505 Manuscript. "The Helmeted Lady." 1p., ink. [This is the title and cast of characters for a play based on the story by Thomas Wood Stevens (signed typed copy attached). The play was not written]

M510 Manuscript. [List of officers and notes taken during a meeting of the Navy Relief Society] 3p. of manuscript plus typed sheets and booklets. No date.

M515 Manuscript. *Ryland*. [An abstract in the hand of KSG] 1p., no date.

Manuscripts. [miscellaneous sheets] :
M520 Pencil manuscript: Cast page for *Caesar's Gods*.
M521 Pencil manuscript: Cast page for an untitled work.
M522 Ink and pencil manuscript: page 3 of an untitled work.

M530 Menu. *Palais de Grub. Cart do Jour.* Dated [in the hand of William O. Goodman] : "Westbrook, Sept. 2nd 1916."

M540 Model Furniture. Five pieces: two chairs, deacon's bench, writing desk, table. Painted cardboard, approx. 1/30 scale. [X]

M550   Newspaper. *The Quotonset Quaff. Perryville, Quotonset Beach, Connecticut.* 4p., no date.

M560   Notebook. Contains one untitled essay about KSG's freshman year at Princeton University. 302p.; 8 fols. are blank.

M570   Notebook.   Contents:

Page
[1]   an ink drawing
[2]   *The seas daughter – a song* (deleted), pencil
[3]   ink drawings
[5]   ink drawing of a man's head
[7] – [13]   *Act II* of an unidentified play. Characters: Ella, Bert.
[17]   *From a rhymers Summer,* pencil
[20]   *The long loved pewter plates* (incomplete), pencil
[20]   *Oh little house that fronts the sea* (incomplete), pencil
[21]   *no flower of passion red or white*, pencil
[21]   *How she must love you! quite as I* (incomplete), pencil
[23]   *How she will love you!* (incomplete), pencil
[23]   *Your rooms must love her* (incomplete), pencil
[36]   *I set my feet upon the hills of spring* (incomplete), pencil

M580   Painting. Exterior of House with Tree. 19¾x24, oil on canvas. Unframed. [his?] [X]

M590   Painting. House at Westbrook. 27¼x27¼, oil on canvas. Framed. [X]

M600   Painting. Westbrook Interior with Flowers. 12x18, oil on board. Framed. [X]

M610   Painting. *My Flower Garden* [Westbrook] . 13x20, oil on board. Framed. [X]

M615   Photograph. Ephraim and the Winged Bear. Note by Thomas Wood Stevens: "Ephraim and the Winged Bear. Produced by Sam Hume, Arts and Crafts Theatre, Detroit." 8x10, no date.

M617   Photograph. The Game of Chess. 8x10, no date.

M620   Photograph. The Parting. Note by Thomas Wood Stevens: "This shows the set, but is not to be published. Proofs of better photographs to follow. T.W.S." 4x9, no date.

M630   Photograph. The Wonder Hat. Note on reverse: Produced by Sam Hume. Arts & Crafts Theatre, Detroit. 6¼x9¼, no date.

M640   Play Bill. Cliff Dwellers' Playhouse. Program: *Symphonie Bacchanale; Overture – Follies of 1812; Mr. Rooster's All-Star Bawl Nine; Italian Coster Singer and his Famous Dancing Bear; Greco-Ballet-Russe; LaFancy Julia del West.* No date.

M645   Play Bill. Gaiety Theatre, Manchester. "A Man Can Only Do His Best . . ." [Premiere Night program, July 6th, 1914]

M650   Postcard. To Kenneth Sawyer Goodman from the Cliff Dwellers. Announcement of performance March 31, 1911.

M660   Printing Plate. Cover for *Caesar's Gods.* Engraved "H.C. Kiefer" in the plate. 3¼x4¾, metal on wood block.

M670   Printing Plate. Cover for *Caesar's Gods.* Engraved "H.C.Kiefer" in the plate. 5x7¼, metal on wood block.

M680   Printing Plate. Cover for *The Masque of Montezuma.* Engraved "Hazel Frazee" in the plate. 4¾x6¾, metal on wood block.

M690   Printing Plate. Cover for *Rainald and the Red Wolf.* Engraved "H.C. Kiefer" in the plate. 5¼x7, metal on wood block.

M701   Printing Plates. Four plates, marked "Scene I,"
M702   "Scene II," "Scene III," and "Scene IV." From *A*
M703   *Pageant for Independence Day.* Each 2¼x3¼, metal
M704   on wood block.

M710   Printing Plate. "From the Library of Kenneth Sawyer Goodman." 1¼x3, metal on wood block.

M720   Printing Plate. "Kenneth Sawyer Goodman, Railway Exchange, Chicago." ¾x3, metal.

M730   Printing Plate. Pair of matched plates of a lamp with decorative border, each 1¼x2½, metal on wood block.

M735   Program. "Herring's Luck or How They Almost Got Two Perfectly Good Husbands. Adapted from the French by Mr. John B. Anderson and Mr. K. Sawyer Goodman." Marked in the hand of KSG: "Given at Saint's Rest. Oct. 16th, 1909 – A great success."

M737   Program. "War Benefit Performance. Henri Durot Master Spy. by Kenneth S. Goodman and Ben Hecht." [The back of the program contains a drawing done in the style of KSG, but not signed] [8] p.

M740   Scrapbook. [Clippings, reviews, papers, etc.] 1910-1917. Unpaged.

M750   Scrapbook. *Hawaii and California, February 9 to April 26, 1913.* [46] p.

M760   Scrapbook. *The Hill School, 1901-1902.* Includes photographs, play bills, signs and letters. [82] p. [X]
Letters:
From John Meigs to William O. Goodman, April 25, 1901
From KSG to Boonie, October 18, 19[?]
From John Meigs to William O. Goodman, November 18, 1901
From John Meigs to KSG, December 28, 1901
From Mrs. Meigs to KSG, January 6, 1902
From John Meigs to William O. Goodman, February 10, 1902
From John Meigs to William O. Goodman, July 11, 1902
From Dwight R. Meigs to KSG, July 5, 19[?]
From Dwight R. Meigs to KSG, June [?], 1902
From John Meigs to William O. Goodman, May 16, 1902
From John Meigs to William O. Goodman, May 2, 1902
From John Meigs to William O. Goodman, December 14, 1901
From Augustus W. Eddy to KSG, August 21, 1902
From KSG to Muff & Boon, May 20, 1902
From John Meigs to William O. Goodman, May 27, 1903
From William O. Goodman to John Meigs, June 1, 1903

M770   Scrapbook. *Joyeuse, January 12 to February 27, 1912.* Photographs, with text by Lawrence Armour. [71] p. [X]

M773   Scrapbooks. *Princeton. 1902-1903, 1903-1904, 1904-1905, 1905-1906, Graduate. K. Sawyer Goodman.* Includes clippings, photographs, correspondence, class programs, contributions of art and writing to campus publications, and a variety of memorabilia (e.g., railroad, sports, and theater tickets, laundry receipts, local business advertisements). 5 vols. [PUL]

M775   Stationery. The Princeton Tiger. Kenneth S. Goodman, Managing Editor. [Back has notes in hand of ? done in or after 1923]

M780   Typescript. *A Masque in Verse [A Singer's Masque]* Called "The Wood of Dreams." This is a version edited by Wallace Rice [?].

M790   Folder. Clippings, play bills, programs and memorabilia about KSG and/ or his plays.

OFFICE OF THE COMMANDANT
U. S. NAVAL TRAINING STATION
GREAT LAKES, ILLINOIS

May 16, 1918.

To: Lieutenant
    Kenneth S. Goodman, USNRF.

    SUBJECT: Orders; temporary duty on board U.S.S. Isla
             de Luzon.

    1. Proceed to the port in which the U.S.S. Isla de
Luzon may be and report to the Commanding Officer thereof for
temporary duty under instruction on board that vessel until on
or about May 28, 1918, when this temporary duty will terminate
at whatever port the U.S.S. Isla De Luzon may be at that time.

    2. Upon the completion of this temporary duty, you
will return to Great Lakes, Illinois.

    3. This is in addition to your present duties.

HWF/A

- -

1st Indorsement.   Office of the Commandant,
                            U.S.Naval Training Station,
                               Great Lakes, Ill.

    1. Received this date.

- -

4th endorsement   Office of Commandant,
                            Naval Training Station,
                              Great Lakes, Illinois,
                                 May 29, 1918.

To: Lieutenant
    Kenneth S. Goodman, USNRF.

    1. Reported return this date.

HWF-B   By direction.

Travel in obedience to these orders was performed as follows:
    Left Detroit, Mich. 11:30 P/M. May 28, 1918
    Arrived Great Lakes, Illinois, 10:00a .m. May 29, 1918.

REVIEW AT GREAT LAKES NAVAL STATION, 1917.
KENNETH SAWYER GOODMAN ON RIGHT,
CHARLES S. DEWEY FAR LEFT,
CAPTAIN W.A. MOFFETT SECOND FROM LEFT

From the Diary of Charles S. Dewey, January 12, 1919:

". . . Just before his [Captain Hutcheson's] *arrival I was shocked to receive a telegram from Great Lakes announcing the death of Kenneth Goodman. Poor old "K". He accompanied the Captain on a trip East, & while there contracted a severe cold which developed into phnewmonia & ended in his death. I will miss him more than I can say as we had so very much in common."*

ADDENDA

P615 *Greeting*
If this, our book, your passing note engages
Bric-a-Brac 30 (1906) p6

M376a Drawings. For the *Princeton Bric-a-Brac*. 1904.
Headpieces:

Page	Title
159	Gymnastic Association
245	Religious Organizations
276	The Indiana Club
292	Valaric Club (undergraduate eating club)
304	Vlanu Club (undergraduate eating club)
349	Directory

M376b Drawings. For the *Princeton Bric-a-Brac*. 1905.
Headpieces:

Page	Title
50	Sophomore Class
119	Baseball
177	The Banjo Club
269	The Sectional Clubs
275	The Indiana Club
304	Alvana Club (undergraduate eating club)

Cartoons:

344-45, 347, 349-52	Retrospect, 7 spots

Designed by Diane L. Backes and composed in
Press Roman with titles in Caxton Roman at
Backes Graphics, Pennington, New Jersey.

Five hundred copies of this book have been printed on
neutralized Writers Offset paper and bound at
Quinn-Woodbine, Inc., Woodbine, New Jersey.

Transfer
Art Dept
May 1992